Toward a Rhetoric of Insult

Toward a Rhetoric of Insult

THOMAS CONLEY

The University of Chicago Press   Chicago and London

THOMAS CONLEY is professor of communication at the
University of Illinois, Urbana-Champaign. He is the author of
Byszantine Culture in Renaissance and Baroque Poland and *Rhetoric
and the European Tradition*, among other publications.

The University of Chicago Press, Chicago 60637
The University of Chicago Press, Ltd., London
© 2010 by The University of Chicago
All rights reserved. Published 2010
Printed in the United States of America

19 18 17 16 15 14 13 12 11   10   1 2 3 4 5

ISBN-13: 978-0-226-11477-4 (cloth)
ISBN-13: 978-0-226-11478-1 (paper)
ISBN-10: 0-226-11477-5 (cloth)
ISBN-10: 0-226-11478-3 (paper)

Library of Congress Cataloging-in-Publication Data

Conley, Thomas, 1941–
    Toward a rhetoric of insult / Thomas Conley.
        p. cm.
    Includes bibliographical references and index.
    ISBN-13: 978-0-226-11477-4 (cloth : alk. paper)
    ISBN-10: 0-226-11477-5 (cloth : alk. paper)
    ISBN-13: 978-0-226-11478-1 (pbk. : alk. paper)
    ISBN-10: 0-226-11478-3 (pbk. : alk. paper)   1. Invective. 2. Rhetoric.
I. Title.
    P410 .I58C66 2010
    808.7—dc22

                                              2009032306

CONTENTS

Preface vii

1 ∗ *The Range of Insult* 1

Terms of Abuse: The Lexical Approach 9
Beyond the Lexicon 13
Nonverbal "Terms" 22
The Problem of the Intrinsic 25

2 ∗ *Traditional Principles of Insult* 31

Sex, Lies, and Rhetorical Community 31
All Those Nauseous Epigrams of Martial 40
The Domestication of Sir John Falstaff 50
"I shall taunt you a second time-a!": Monty Python 61
Just Add a Dash of Theology 69
Lines and Storylines 78
Doing the Dozens 87
Mind Your Manners 91
Insults as "Rhetoric" 93

3 ∗ *Beyond "Traditional" Rhetoric* 97

The Paradox of Insult 97
The Economics of Shame 99
Maintaining vs. Interrogating Hierarchies 101
Enforcing "Civility" 113
The Aesthetic Angle 117
Ad bellum purificandum? 119
A Parting Shot 126

Notes for Further Reading 127
Index 131

PREFACE

This brief essay grew out of my frustration at having no general treatment of the subject to recommend to my students in a course on the rhetoric of insults. So I decided to do something about that and collect some thoughts I have on the subject. This volume is brief because nothing much would be gained simply by providing more, and longer, examples of what is a universal cultural practice.

The main idea I have centers on the suggestion I want to develop here that consideration of the practice of insult or vituperation might benefit from taking a rhetorical perspective on it. This has, to my knowledge, never been done before—at least not in an organized and relatively comprehensive way. I say "relatively comprehensive" because the particularities of insult are almost infinite, and so not much more than a beginning to consideration of the subject is feasible.

But what a rhetorical perspective brings out is that insult can be seen as at once "antisocial" and constitutive of social relations. That is, there is a "benign" side to insults as well as a "malign" side. As we proceed, we will find ourselves poaching on territory claimed by a variety of other fields and disciplines—lexicography, social and linguistic anthropology, literary criticism, history, and art criticism, among them—and with broader questions of interpretation of both words and actions. There is considerable overlap, for instance, between insults and irony, and problems of interpretation common to both. I will not spend much time on such questions beyond drawing attention to their relevance. What I am concerned to do here is not to "theorize" insult, but simply to find a way to organize a discussion of this subject along the lines of a notion of rhetoric conceived, as many will quickly recognize, with Kenneth Burke's *Rhetoric of Motives* in mind. And I hope that such a discussion will both point up various aspects of insult that

have not been very carefully attended to and stimulate some constructive conversation about this most human of human behaviors.

Some of the examples I have provided in the body of the present
text come from presentations by students in the Rhetoric of Insults
course over the past couple of years. My main debts are to Steve Bethel,
Brian Blum, Sara Edelstein, Elizabeth Foste, Ed Laube, Michelle Lit-
teken, Bob Taliana, and Emily West. I want also to express my gratitude
to WittyWorld Books and Capp Enterprises Inc. for permission to use
copyrighted materials and, especially, to Amy Holland and my wife,
Elizabeth, for assistance with technical matters.

Urbana, Illinois, May 2009

CHAPTER 1

The Range of Insult

In late December 2006, Ilan Greenberg reported in the *New York Times* (December 24, 2006) that an article "seen as denigrating Islam" published in an obscure Baku newspaper "prompted demonstrations across Azerbaijan and in Iran." The article blamed Islam for Azerbaijan's sluggish economic development, and the demonstrations raised concern over Iran's influence in that country. An Iranian cleric demanded the death of the authors of the article, Greenberg reported, "and other religious conservatives in Azerbaijan have sent tremors through the Azeri government." Quoted in the article was an imam at one of the more prestigious mosques in Baku, Haji Ilgar, who is reported to have said, "I am for freedom of speech, but not the freedom to insult."

This was, at the time, the most recent of several stories I saw in the news during 2006 that featured "insult" that gave rise to indignation, anger, civil unrest, and even deaths. There was another story in the *Times* earlier in the year (July 10, 2006, in an article by Judy Dempsey). At what is described in the article as "a low point for Poland's relations with Europe," Polish president Lech Kaczynski cancelled a summit meeting with German chancellor Angela Merkel and French president Jacques Chirac, evidently (according to "senior Polish diplomats and opposition politicians") because of a satirical article in the German newspaper *Taz* that said of Kaczynski that the only thing he knows about Germany "is the spittoon in the men's toilet at Frankfurt Airport," and described him and his twin brother, Jaroslav, as "the Polish new potatoes." Poland's foreign minister, Anna Fotyga, demanded a formal apology by the German Foreign Ministry, but got none—a response she described as "shocking," since the language of the article could be compared to language used in *Der Stürmer*, a propaganda weekly during the Nazi era. The immediate result of all this was considerable damage, in the view of many prominent Polish politicians, to Poland's interests—not to mention considerable public uproar in both Poland and Germany. A subsequent report (*New York Times*, August 7, 2006) by the *International Herald Tribune*'s Andreas Tzortzis clarifies the matter. The original headline in *Tageszeitung* ("*Taz*," for short) was "Poland's New Potatoes: Rogues Who Want to Rule the World," and the article ended with the assertion that Jaroslaw Kaczynski still lived with his mother, "but at least without a marriage certificate." And there were several other printed slights, enough to make one think that 2006 may have been "The Year of Global Insult."

"Insult," then, is evidently seen as a sign of fractures or fissures in social and political civility that give rise to turmoil and conflict. There is a wealth of literature devoted to "conflict management" in both business settings and international diplomacy. And much has been written about "civility" recently (e.g., by Charles Taylor, by the "communitarians," by those debating the question of "public space" or, indeed, whether there is a "public," and so forth); but little attention has been paid to the culprit in all the failures to preserve or encourage civility—insults.

If you look around for systematic examinations of what it is that constitutes an insult, you will find that insult or insulting behavior remains one of the most overlooked (although not unnoticed) and underexamined features of everyday social interaction. Examine available research databases, for instance, and you will find little in the way of general considerations of the ways in which insults are universal among humans gathered together, and even less about why they are so universal. There is plenty of data, a very long and diverse story of social experience, but not much reflection on what that data can—or should—teach us. This book, without going into an elaborate justification-cum-survey of "the state of the art," is intended to make a start on such reflection.

There are, of course, some questions of enormous range and importance that such reflection might turn up. But let us begin with a simpler and more mundane kind of question: what do we mean when we call something an "insult"? Most often—and I am not claiming that this is particularly rigorous (or original)—we mean that it is an expression of a severely negative opinion of a person or group in order to subvert their positive self-regard and esteem; and often we consider insults to be examples of verbal abuse. It's clear, for instance, that a remark such as "You've got a face that would gag a maggot" is an insult. Fine. But not very enlightening. To begin with, consider the range of synonyms for "insult" in English that come to mind: "slighting," "affront," "ridicule," "malediction," "vituperation," "invective," "contumely," "mocking"; or, at a more vernacular level, "name-calling," "roasting," "put-down."

All of these, of course, have very different connotations, and these connotations in turn suggest a number of different dimensions along which "insult" can be plotted. Just a few of these dimensions—and again, I am not claiming rigorous analysis here—include what might be called "scenario," "intensity," and "vehicle." "Scenario" can be conceived in both "horizontal" and "vertical" terms. "You've got a face that would gag a maggot" or the Shakespearean "Thou puking, toad-spotted maltworm," for instance, are remarks probably made by an individual to another individual—perhaps the most common scenario that comes to mind. But insults can be directed by an individual against a group—the evangelizing preacher who comes to my campus, for instance, and addresses his gathered student audience as "a bunch of whores and drunks"; or one of Aristophanes' characters (Dikaiopolis in the *Acharnians* comes to mind) berating members of the assembly or the chorus. The converse scenario is also common: a group insulting an individual. Think of a theatre audience heckling an actor on stage. And of course there are insults directed by one group against another: the supporters of a losing college football team chanting to the supporters of their more powerful opposition, "That's all right. That's OK. You will work for us some day!" or the English soccer hooligans to the Germany fans across the stadium, "We beat you in '45, Fritz, and we'll beat you Nazis today!" Notice that some of these are exchanges between equal parties, and some are levied by (purported) superiors to inferiors or inferiors to superiors. This is the "vertical" dimension I referred to earlier. Both horizontal and vertical exchanges may be sanctioned or not: saying to someone, "You smell so bad, the last time you took a bath the soap fainted" or "Yo' mama so ugly she hurts my feelings" is permitted by the conventions governing "The Dozens," as the invective in Aristophanes was sanctioned by the conventions of Old Comedy; and indeed, it is said that it is mandatory in castebound Indian society for an Untouchable to insult himself when addressing a member of a higher caste. By contrast, what most would see as unwarranted slurs or name-calling beyond the bounds of "good taste" are, precisely, unwarranted by good taste—viz., not sanctioned, so in violation of common norms of decorum. Examples of the latter are myriad, and we will see a great many more as we proceed. For the present, one final remark should be made about "scenario," and that is that considerations of scenario (or setting, or situation) are absolutely fundamental to our understanding of insult. About this, too, we shall have much to say.

Subverting someone's self-esteem may get one in trouble. Insult people, and you will likely hurt their feelings—and that usually evokes a reaction. If someone's self-esteem is sufficiently subverted by an insult, the reaction can be violent—a punch in the face or even a duel in some societies. One group's insults against another group can result in riot (think of the reactions in the spring of 2006 to the Danish cartoons depicting Mohammed), diplomatic crisis, or even war. So the matter of "intensity," of a scale of "hurt," comes into consideration—in both sanctioned and unsanctioned insults. This, too, turns up a dazzling variety of possibilities. For instance, some insulting behavior is regarded as not serious, but entertaining. Many an afternoon has been passed in an Irish pub enjoying "the *craik*," banter between friends that often verges on—but never quite becomes—serious malediction. There are many club comedians whose schtick is audience abuse, whether discomforting (think of the old Lenny Bruce) or reassuring (as in the recent rash of "blue collar" or "redneck" acts). Or consider the ways in which characters in a situation comedy (*Seinfeld* comes to mind) sometimes actually strengthen their bonds with one another through insults. By contrast, sometimes "making fun" of another can result in genuine hurt feelings (which in turn can vary from "I'm rubber, you're glue. Whatever you say bounces off me and sticks to you" to angry tears—and more); and sometimes sanctioned entertaining insults end up cutting to the quick (as, for instance, when insulting remarks during a political roast may be acutely embarrassing because true). So what was intended to be entertaining turns out to be serious. This raises another dimension of insult bearing on intensity: the true-not true dimension. On the one hand, to say, in "doing the dozens," "Yo' mama's ass is so big, when she walks down the street it looks like two bears rasslin' under a blanket" is clearly not to make a statement of fact (one hopes), but it is just as clearly meant as an insult. On the other, there are some neighborhoods in Amsterdam, for instance, where to call someone a "whore" is simply to get that person's profession right. If you call an obese person "Fatty," you may intend to insult, but you report in the process a matter of fact. How serious or entertaining an intended insult may be taken to be may also, as the earlier examples suggest, be a matter of whether there are spectators present or not, and of what those spectators expect to hear or see. In short, intensity, as well as the question of whether a given response to a perceived insult is fitting or disproportionate, is always a matter of applicability and expectation—which brings us back again, obviously, to scenario or situation.

A good example of the interplay between intensity and situation can be seen in the transcript of the 1969 Chicago Seven trial that resulted from the demonstrations in Chicago that took place during the 1968 Democratic National Convention. The alleged ringleaders of the demonstrations, Abbie Hoffman, Jerry Rubin, David Dellinger, Rennie Davis, Tom Hayden, John Froines, and Lee Weiner (Bobby Seals was one of the originally indicted, but his trial was separated from that of the others) were charged with conspiracy to incite, and actually inciting, riot under the antiriot provisions of the 1968 Civil Rights Act. The trial lasted for months, resulting in the conviction (which was later reversed) of five of the seven defendants not only on the original charges but on over 150 counts of contempt of court that resulted from repeated exchanges between the defendants and the judge, Julius Hoffman, such as the following (from the transcript of the trial from February 4, 1970, available online at http://www.law.umkc.edu/faculty/projects/ftrials/Chicago7/Chi7_trial.html):

MR. SCHULTZ [prosecuting attorney]: Did Dellinger say anything when this announcement was made?

WITNESS: I did not hear him say anything.

MR. SCHULTZ: Did you see where he went?

WITNESS: He left with the head of the group that were carrying the flags.

MR. DELLINGER: Oh, bullshit. That is an absolute lie!

THE COURT [i.e., Judge Hoffman]: Did you get that, Miss Reporter?

MR. DELLINGER: You're a snake. We have to try to put you in jail for ten years for telling lies about us, Dick Schultz.

MARSHAL JONESON: Be quiet, Mr. Dellinger.

MR. DELLINGER: When it's all over, the judge will go to Florida, but if he has his way, we'll go to jail. That is what we're fighting for, not just for us, but for all the rest of the people in the country who are being oppressed.

VOICES: Right on, right on!

THE COURT: Take that man into custody, Mr. Marshal. Take that man into custody.

MR. SCHULTZ: Into custody?

THE COURT: Into custody.

VOICES: Right on!

MR. DAVIS: Go ahead, Dick Schultz, put everybody in jail.

MR. DELLINGER: Dick Schultz is a Nazi if I ever knew one.

MR. SCHULTZ: Your Honor, will you please tell Mr. Davis to walk away from me?

MR. DELLINGER: Put everybody in jail.

THE COURT: Mr. Davis, will you take your chair.

MR. HOFFMAN: Nazi jailer!

MR. DAVIS: This court is bullshit. . . .

MR. HOFFMAN: You are a disgrace to the Jews. You would have served Hitler better. Dig it!

THE MARSHAL: That was Mr. Hoffman, your Honor.

THE COURT: I saw him and I heard him.

MR. RUBIN: You are a fascist! Hoffman . . .

THE MARSHAL: Clear the court!

Disorder in the court, to be sure. Defendants speaking up out of turn, spectators chiming in, and name-calling—clearly "contempt of court." But notice the insults here. Schultz is called a "snake" and a "Nazi"; the court is called "bullshit"; and the judge is called a "fascist" and a "Nazi." But "snake" is pretty mild, and "bullshit" is not much more than a barnyard epithet. And "fascist" and "Nazi" are terms that were, in those days (and perhaps even today), bandied about with stupefying abandon. But this, after all, was a federal trial with its rules for procedure and courteous behavior. And judge Julius Hoffman was, of course, a prestigious federal judge—and a Jew.

In addition to drawing attention to the connection between scenario and intensity, this also brings us to the third consideration, what I am calling "vehicle," or perhaps "medium." It is probably safe to say that when we think of insults, we think of something someone *says* to another; so the most common—but certainly not, as we shall see, the exclusive—vehicle for insult is verbal. Verbal insult ranges from terms or phrases "of abuse" uttered by themselves to statements (such as the one about "rasslin'" bears) to the more complex articulations that one finds in slogans, ditties, poems of various lengths, extended passages of invective, and satires (Swift's *Mechanical Operations of the Spirit*, for instance), and so on. We can find in every language, and in the literature of every language, a rich repertoire of terms of abuse and genres of insult, from street ditties ("Little Johnny Deveroo, we don't want to play with you / It's not because you're dirty, it's not because you're clean / It's because you are a Protestant and eat margareen" was popular in my old neighborhood) to ancient Greek iambics, Nordic and Scottish flyting, and the satires of Juvenal and Old Comedy—to name just a few. The subject of "terms of abuse" is fascinating and so broad as to deserve separate treatment (see the section that follows). But for now it may be enough to observe that, to borrow some terms from the old rhetorical tradition, it is not only the *elocutio* (diction, style) of insults that demands attention but also, and perhaps more importantly, the delivery (*pronuntiatio*)—tone of voice, volume, tenor, body language (facial expression, gestures of the eye, posture, and the like), and, above all, timing. These elements are impossible to treat adequately in a book like this, and so will not receive the attention that they deserve. But it is important to note that insults involve not only verbal resources but nonverbal or paraverbal resources as well. In fact, a great many vehicles for insult are exclusively nonverbal. Inappropriate attire, bad table manners, a patronizing tone of voice—not to mention the obscene gestures we are all familiar with, like mooning—are all ways of insulting others. What keeps the verbal and nonverbal methods in the same category is the fact that they are both varieties of what Kenneth Burke so famously called "symbolic action." Accordingly, when we look in the next section at terms of abuse, we shall have some observations to make on nonverbal as well as verbal "terms."

But there is one final observation to make about vehicles. Looking at verbal terms of abuse, we will see that there appear to be few—if any—

terms that are inherently abusive, that is, insulting. What counts as a term of abuse will vary from language to language and from culture to culture; and even within one language, a given term (obviously) can be (or not be) abusive or can be more or less abusive depending on—again—the situation. Even more complicated are the specific gestures or manners of conduct that are considered insulting, depending on which culture one is considering. There is, so to speak, no lexicon that will tell you that a given behavior is inherently or situationally insulting, since most of what is considered insulting (or, for that matter, acceptable or laudable) behavior is so deeply rooted in a host of social and cultural practices and competencies as to defy explanation, much less easy interpretation. Which is to say: when we approach symbolic action at a cultural level, we are immersing ourselves in matters of "situation" that are so deep and complicated as to be, in the end, inexplicable.

Our discussion of vehicle would be sadly incomplete if we did not mention another common vehicle for insult: cartoon drawings, the components of which include caricature, usually by exaggeration of physical characteristics or dress, and the judgment being rendered. The power of cartoons as insults was clearly demonstrated in the publication of the Danish newspaper cartoons depicting Mohammed and the consequent riots in Pakistan and Indonesia (and elsewhere) that we mentioned earlier. While those cartoons may not have been intended as much more than wry commentary—in one, Mohammed exclaims to a line of suicide bombers outside the gates of paradise, "Stop! We've run out of virgins!"—they were perceived in Islamic regions as vile insults of the Prophet, virtual blasphemy. In this respect, they might be viewed in the context of a long tradition in Europe of cartoons that were indeed meant to offend "the opposition" while they served to define a sense of community among those whose position they were meant to represent. Examples of this class of insult can be found among, for instance, cartoons in British publications (and not just in the nineteenth century) depicting semihuman Irish; or World War II–era depictions of Japanese or Germans that were part of the propaganda campaigns of the time; or even of the tamer political cartoons by the likes of Herblock more recently. We will have occasion to look at some of these later. But here it can be said that the ability to "get" such cartoons involves an ability to decode visual symbols that is every bit as complex as the ability to know an insulting gesture—and to gauge its intensity—when one sees one.

Terms of Abuse: The Lexical Approach

I once conducted an informal survey, asking twenty-eight students in my class (all of them native English speakers) to list ten insulting terms they could think of, in no particular order. I urged them not to be shy, and to indicate only their gender. The results were more interesting than I expected, even though the terms they listed were not. For one thing, the categories of abuse split almost evenly between male and female students. Females listed mainly terms having to do with physical appearance ("fat" and "ugly" at the top); and male students mainly listed terms concerning sexual orientation ("fag," for instance). Both males and females listed terms having to do with intelligence—or lack of it—such as "jerk," "idiot," "asshole," and the like. One set of terms that was conspicuously absent were animal terms—"pig," "rat," "dirty dog," and the like ("bitch" appeared on a few lists, but it had little to do with actual dogs). What was most striking, however, was the semantic poverty of their lists. At ten terms per student and twenty-eight students, the grand total of terms had the potential to reach 280 items. But the students came up with pretty much the same dozen or so terms that they agreed were insulting—and some of them could not even come up with ten terms! In a later session in which I reported the results, I pointed out that, by contrast, Robert Édouard's *Dictionnaire des injures* (Paris, 1979) lists almost three thousand terms of abuse. And that is only in the *domaine française*!

We will see some of the terms in Édouard shortly. (One of the interesting things about Édouard's list is the large number of terms and phrases that concern driving and automobiles.) For now, I wish to point out that making lists of terms of abuse is an almost impossible task. While it may be true that some terms seem patently abusive— "jerk" or "asshole," for instance—a second look often shows that not to be the case. In fact, there seem to be no terms, in English or in any other language I know something about, that are *inherently* abusive. Also—and this may be a result of our previous observation—the list of terms that are potentially abusive and, of those terms, that context shows are clearly intended to be abusive is very long, very complicated, and often puzzling. And, finally, abusive language can be found in almost any member of the vast family of human modes and genres of expression—sometimes where one would not expect to find it. A striking example of this can be located in the works of early Latin Church Fathers! In Ilona Opelt's *Die Polemik in der christlichen lateinischen Literatur von Tertullian bis Augustin* (Heidelberg, 1980), we find a twenty-page index of Latin terms of abuse containing about 1,400 terms. Accordingly, the only way to proceed at this point is to work inductively and see if any commonalities or other patterns can be detected. And accordingly, too, what follows is pitifully incomplete, as the pool of abuse is very deep and wide. But let us begin.

Since I have already mentioned Édouard's *Dictionnarie*, let us begin with some of the terms he lists:

andouille	*cruche*	*omelette*
âne	*dingo*	*pamplemousse*
babouin	*éléphant*	*plafond*
bécheur	*fignard*	*puce*
cochon	*fléau*	*putain*
con	*hareng*	*singe*
crapule	*imbécile*	*sot*
crétin	*maraud*	*teigne*
crotte	*monstre*	*tocard*

A number of these need little in the way of translation: *crétin, monstre, imbécile, éléphant*, and perhaps *putain* ("whore") and *maraud* ("rogue," as in "marauder"). The appearance of "elephant" alerts us to other animal terms in this list (which, as short as it is, is hardly statistically representative), some of them with obvious English equivalents: *âne* ("ass"), *babouin* ("baboon"), *cochon* ("pig"), *dingo* ("dingo"), *hareng* ("herring"), *singe* ("monkey"), *puce* ("flea"), and *teigne* ("moth," but in some contexts "ringworm"!). There are a couple of "generic" terms: *con*, which is hard to translate but means, roughly, "dummy"; and *sot* ("stupid"); and some more vivid and particular: *fléau* ("plague"), *plafond* ("deranged," someone with his head in the clouds), *tocard* ("ugly"), *crapule* ("drunk," as in "crapulent"), and *cruche* ("fool," but literally "jug"). Even more intense are *fignard* ("asshole," sometimes with connotations of constipation) and *crotte* ("turd"—but a *crotte de chocolate* is a chocolate drop!). And we have some odd ones: *andouille* is, of course, a kind of sausage, but it also means "imbecile"; a *pamplemousse* is a grapefruit, but means "fatso"; and *omelette* means "omelette," of course, but also means "wimp."

We will try to sort these terms out later to see if there are any patterns that emerge. But let us turn now to another language, Polish. For this I have consulted a little book entitled *Dictionary of Polish Obscenities* by (what is surely a nom de plume) Stanislaw Kielbasa (Oakland, CA, 1978, and frequently reprinted), since my own grasp of Polish terms of abuse is the result of sitting around in Polish taverns in Chicago and is therefore not up to the standard of academic rigor necessary here. To offer just a sample of what we find in Kielbasa (which, by the way, is a kind of sausage and accordingly slang for *membrum virile*, for which there are countless synonyms in English): *chamka* (HAM-ka—with a hard *h*—"slut"), *dupa* (DOO-pa, "ass," the body part), *dupsko* ("big ass"), *dziwa* (DJEEV-a, "slut"), *kiep* (KEE-ep, "jerk"), *pedał* (PED-aw, "queer"), *skubany* (sku-BAN-ee, "bastard," "son of a bitch"), and the list goes on. Polish has many rather creative terms of abuse, as in, for instance, *chomąto* (kho-MAN-tow, "hick," literally "horse collar"), *dziobak* (djee-YO-bak, "queer," literally "platypus"!), *franca* (FRAN-cha, "ugly woman," literally "syphilitic"), *deska* ("woman with a small bosom," literally "board"), *wydra* (VEE-dra, "nympho," literally "otter"), *chuju rybi* (HOO-yoo RIB-ee, "fish's prick"), and so on. If this sample seems overly concerned with sexual organs and orientations, bear in mind that Kielbasa is listing obscenities. Poles are able to insult more than just matters pertaining to sexual behavior.

A few terms appear in Kielbasa that have Yiddish counterparts—to be expected, given the large number of loanwords in Yiddish: *szmata* (SHMAT-a, "slut," literally "rag") and *śiksa* (SHIK-sa, also "slut," but in Yiddish often a less severe "non-Jewish woman"). Many Yiddish terms of abuse have entered into broader public discourse, as Leo Rosten's *The Joys of Yiddish* (New York, 1968) makes clear: *shmo* ("an unlucky fool"), for instance, or *dreck* ("worthless trash"), or *schlemiel* and *shlimazel* (roughly, "born loser," but often with a subtle difference). As one classic distinction puts it, "A *shlemiel* is the guy who always spills his soup; a *shlimazel* is the guy he spills it on"). A little less widely known, perhaps, are such terms as *klutz* ("clumsy person"), *pisher* (literally "a bed wetter," so "a nobody"), *yenta* ("an interfering older woman"), *kvetcher* ("whiner"), *nebbech/ nebbish* ("loser") or *shmuck* (from the German for "embellishment" or "decoration," but slang for "penis" and, by extension, "a prick"; compare *putz*). Woody Allen movies abound in such terms. To these we might add, for instance, *yekl* ("sucker"), *shnorrer* ("cheapskate," "bum"), *bulbenik* ("clumsy person"), *alter kocker* ("old fart"), *meshuggener* ("crazy person"), *momzer* (literally a bastard child, hence "detestable person"), *gonif* ("thief"), *shikker* ("drunk"), and *chozzer* (literally "pig," so someone who is greedy).

One point that emerges immediately is that even a brief and sketchy review is enough to show that languages generally have enormous repositories of terms of abuse. There is no shortage of such terms. Accordingly, it looks as though we might imagine a huge, multilingual thesaurus of abuse. Words for "fool" or "jerk" seem to abound. But, bearing in mind our earlier observations about applicability, appropriateness, and intensity, some caution is clearly in order. For one thing, one would have to be absolutely fluent in the various languages our thesaurus would include, or else blunders would be inevitable—not just lexical blunders but social blunders as well. This is, of course, just as true for a nonnative speaker of English consulting a dictionary of American slang (of which there are several in circulation), who would without a doubt miss many of the nuances of slang expressions—indeed, who might not be able to distinguish a term that is used metaphorically from one that is not.

That brings us to a second point, which is that the language of abuse is rich in stylistic potential—and I mean by "stylistic" something very like the traditional elements of style, such as tropes and figures. Look at how many terms in our list from Édouard are metaphors, not only animal terms, such as *âne*, *puce*, or *teigne*, but also *andouille*, *omelette*, and *pamplemousse*. And as far as metaphors are concerned, what of the Polish *dziobak* or *wydra*, *szmata* or *chomąto*? Some of our terms qualify as instances also of synecdoche: *fignard*, for instance, or *shmuck*. It might be added that, as common and important as synecdoches of abuse are in verbal language, they may be even more common and important in the visual rhetoric of caricatures and cartoons. For hyperbole, we might look to *éléphant* or the Polish *franca*.

Hyperbolic terms of abuse might seem by nature to be more intense than others. But in themselves their intensity is largely a matter of situation or scenario. There are, in any case, more ways to intensify an insult than choosing hyperbolic terms. We have, in English, a host of semantic or lexical markers to indicate intensity. To say to someone, "You are a pig" is one thing. To say, in colloquial English, "You're some kind of pig" or "You are nothing but a pig" is another. To say, "You Hindu!" is one thing—and maybe not even an insult. To say "You fuckin' Hindu!" is to say something else, and definitely an insult. The simplest way to intensify an insult is by means of the old figure, *accumulatio*, i.e., to pile one abusive term upon another, as, for instance, in the lines given by Shakespeare to Kent early in the second act of *King Lear*, where he sums up another character as

> A knave, a rascal, an eater of broken meats; a base, proud, shallow, beggarly three-suited, hundred-pound, filthy, worsted-stocking knave; a lily-livered, action-taking knave; a whoreson, glass-gazing, superserviceable, finical rogue . . . nothing but the composition of a knave, beggar, coward, pander, and the son and heir of a mongrel bitch. (2.2.15–24)

We will see many more instances of such "piling on" before we are finished, but for now it may be sufficient to heed the warning that it is not always the case that "more is better." Accumulated insults often turn out to be more awkward than abusive—particularly, as we shall soon see, if they are not coherent. But perhaps the most effective ways call for more elaborate stylistic displays using several resources at once, as in the assessment made by a British critic of the author of a book under review, describing him as "a balding, bug-eyed opportunist with the looks of a punctured beach ball, the charisma of a glove puppet, and an ego the size of a Hercules supply plane. And I speak as a friend."

Beyond the Lexicon

The original treasury of abuse in Latin literature was put together by the comic playwrights Plautus and Terence. A partial survey of the terms we find in their plays reveals some patterns familiar to us from our earlier look at terms from seldom-taught languages, but Roman comedy has more to offer yet. (I have depended heavily on Saara Lilja's monograph [based on her Helsinki dissertation] *Terms of Abuse in Roman Comedy*, Annales Academiae Scientiarum Fennicae, Ser. B, no. 141:3 (Helsinki, 1965). Lilja, of course, gives the older Latin orthography.)

We can, I think, pass over the most common and obvious terms: *inprobus* ("perverse" or, less severely, "naughty") and *inpudens* ("impudent," more literally, "shameless"); or *malus* ("wicked") and its superlative, *pessumus*; or *scelus* ("scoundrel") and its many derivatives. And there are some terms that are fairly obviously meant to be abusive: *audax* (compare *inpudens*); *bardus* ("stupid"; compare the also common *stultus*); *carnifex* ("scoundrel," but also "tormentor" or "hangman," its basic meaning); *edentulus* ("toothless"); *insanus* ("feeble," but also close to "insane"); *monstrum*; *nequam* ("worthless"); *scurra* ("buffoon"); *vetulus* ("old fart"); various variations on *stercus* ("turd"), e.g., *stercoreus*; and the like. The characters in these plays often employ animal terms in their insults: *belua*, for instance, generally means "large beast," but is sometimes used of elephants specifically; and we also find, e.g., *cuculus* ("cuckoo"), *culex* ("gnat"), *hircus* ("goat"); and *lepus* ("hare"). More interesting are various derivative terms: the phrase *clurinum pecus* puts together *clurinum* ("having to do with an ape") with *pecus* ("animal"), the result being something like "apeish critter"; a *furcifer* is, literally, "a carrier of talons," but is also used to mean "gallows bird"; and a *pultiphagus* is a "porridge-eater." Related are terms that are rather metaphorical in nature: *caudex* ("treetrunk") can be translated "blockhead"; and a *mastigia* is one who deserves the lash (from the Greek μαστιγία), hence, "scoundrel." And some instances of abusive language are abusive only because the character using it is being ironic or sarcastic, turning "positive" terms into insults: e.g., *amator* ("lover"), *bonus* (as in "good man"), *fortis* ("strong"), *gloriosus* ("famous"), and the like.

A number of insults in Roman comedy have to do with ethnicity and class. *Barbarus* and *rusticus*, for instance, concern both. The former is from the Greek, and does not mean "barbarian" as much as it does "uncivilized"; and the latter extends beyond mere "rusticity" to denote a "shitkicker" or "hillbilly." Among these, we must also count as meant to be insulting the occasional *mulier* (woman).

We shall look more closely at insults based on ethnicity, class, and gender in due course. For the present, we need to remind ourselves of what we said earlier about the question of "inherently abusive" terms. One of the things our survey here brings out is the necessity of taking into account—not only in the case of drama, but particularly there—who says what about whom and why. *Bonus* and *mulier* are hardly inherently abusive, but they are sometimes used to abuse.

This last observation brings out the limits of a purely lexicographical approach to terms of abuse, the limits of which are brought out, most clearly, I think, by some Internet sites that bill themselves as the "Shakespearean Insult Generator" (http://www.purity.com/websiphon/demos/insulter/) and the "Shakespeare Insult Kit" (http://www.pangloss.com/seidel/shake_rule.html). The Shakespeare Insult Kit consists of three fifty-word lists: (A) simple modifier, (B) complex modifier, and (C) substantive. To give an idea of how it is set up (the examples are drawn from the site):

A	B	C
artless	base-court	apple-john
bawdy	bat-fowling	baggage
beslubbering	beef-witted	barnacle

. . . and so on, down to (A) yeasty, (B) weather-bitten, (C) wagtail. Combine terms from A, B, and C, and you have a Shakespearean insult, for example, "lumpish fool-born clotpole," or "puny milk-livered lout," or "froward dizzy-eyed harpy," or "bootless beef-witted miscreant."

Some potential users of this kit may run into problems, however. Among the substantives listed in column C are, e.g., "bum-bailey," "clack-dish," "fustilarian," "giglet," "mammet," "puttock," and "gudgeon"—and, for that matter, "clotpole" from the earlier example. These words may be found in Shakespeare, but for most would-be insulters, a visit to the OED is in order before trying to generate an insult. Moreover, once one has mastered the meanings of such terms, another problem arises. In many cases, combining items from A, B, and C results in gibberish. Again taking examples from the posted lists, what is one to make of such a Shakespearean insult as "roguish milk-livered bum-bailey"? A "bum-bailey" is (evidently) a cricket, and it is hard to see what a roguish cricket, much less a rogue who is "milk-livered" (compare "lily-livered"), might possibly be. Or what of a "mewling dizzy-eyed bladder"? What on earth is a dizzy-eyed bladder? And how can bladders mewl? In other words, there are what might be called "category inconsistencies" that produce insults that are simply absurd. That may explain why none of the insults we produced by combining column items ever appears in Shakespeare—and indeed it is not clear that any combination yielded by the kit was actually used by Shakespeare. It certainly leaves no room for instances of insult in the opening scene of *Coriolanus*, for instance, in which the revolutionary Caius Marcius, who would later be called "Coriolanus," characterizes the common citizens of Rome as "curs, / that like not peace nor war." "The one affrights you," he continues,

> The other makes you proud. He that trusts to you,
> Where he should find you lions, finds you hares,
> Where foxes, geese. You are no surer, no,
> Than is the coal of fire upon the ice,
> Or hailstone in the sun.
>   (1.1.172–78)

We do not find "curs" or "hares" or "geese" or "hailstones in the sun" in any of the columns that comprise the kit.

An even more serious problem arises when we consider that, even if we were to come up with what looks like a potent insult, for instance, "[Thou art a] puking plume-plucked puttock"—a "puttock" is a buzzard, so it makes sense; and there's artful alliteration involved, too— such an insult would not always be equally applicable to any character in Shakespeare, or, for that matter, to many people you would like to insult. To call Falstaff a "flax-wench" or a "giglet" (a saucy or wanton maid) makes absolutely no sense.

That is, unless somehow the speaker and the setting make calling him a "giglet" intelligible, not to mention insulting. This is a problem that also burdens Web sites and print anthologies that catalog which insults are delivered by which characters in Shakespeare's plays. It may be pretty obvious that Kent's "You whoreson culliony barber-monger" or "You cowardly rascal. Nature disclaims in thee; a tailor made thee" in *King Lear* are (meant to be) insults. But what of Don Pedro's "He doth indeed show some sparks that are like wit" in *Much Ado about Nothing?* Unless one knows why and to whom such things are said and, perhaps more importantly, why we should care, we cannot easily discern the insults. (To her credit, the body of Saara Lilja's dissertation on Roman comedy provides just that sort of information—as does Édouard, over five hundred pages of it.) The *Lear* examples, for instance, are from the same scene in the play (2.2) in which Kent, one of Lear's only supporters, assails Oswald, the errandboy of the devious Goneril. And Don Pedro's quip (at 2.3.192–93)—of Benedick—is not particularly insulting at all. And we are not told these things. As a result, the promise held forth by the subtitle of one of the more popular anthologies of Shakespearean insults (*Shakespeare's Insults*, ed. Wayne F. Hall and Cynthia J. Öttchen [New York, 1995]), "Educating Your Wit," is nothing short of false advertising.

Moving to more immediately familiar ground, we might turn to a large family of terms of abuse current in twentieth-century English dealing with social deviance and sexual and ethnic identity. This is a subject that has attracted considerable attention over the past decades, and I make no attempt here to be nearly exhaustive. But the following, while it breaks no new ground, should remind us all of how common terms of abuse are in everyday popular English.

We have a great many terms to denote, for instance, people who drink to excess. "Drunk" is perhaps the most obvious, but consider also such terms as "alkie," "wino," "rummy," "boozer," "booze-hound," "lush," "soak," "sot," "souse," and the like ("pot-walloper," to my knowledge, is an Irish expression). For drug abusers, too, there are many familiar terms: "junkie," "doper," "user," "cokehead," "pothead," "hophead"— indeed, "head" by itself—and so forth. There are also many terms used of homosexuals (some of the following are not very common these days): "homo," "gay," "fag" (or "faggot"), "pansy," "queer," "fairy," "fruit," or "queen"; "ponce" or calling someone "bent," a "bugger," "sod," or "poof" (British), and "girly-man"; or, on the other side, "dyke," "bulldyke," "butch," or "lesbo." But these, as countless recent studies have detailed, pale by comparison with language commonly used to refer to women generally and to various races or nationalities.

Without making any attempt to be exhaustive (again), it seems that even "girl" can be seen as a term of abuse (compare *mulier* in our list from Roman comedy. Some feminists have objected to the word "*history*" as covertly sexist, but that is another story). There is no doubt that "broad," "chick," "bird," "fox," "vixen," "bitch," "babe," "doll," "sweetie-pie," "cow," "sow," "kitten," "tart," "slut," "floozy," or the more anatomically graphic "cunt," "pussy," "piece" (of "ass"), "snatch," "twat," "lay," "screw," and the like are meant to be "terms of art" when it comes to making derogatory references to females. Some of the terms in English go back to Elizabethan times, or even to Old and Middle English, but occasionally appear in our own time. "Whore" (which goes back to Anglo-Saxon times) is the obvious example, but we sometimes hear "wench," "harlot," "slattern," "shrew," "hag," and, less frequently perhaps, "hussy," "strumpet," "trollop," and "tomato." Terms such as "dish," "vamp," "moll," "cookie," or, in a very different vein, "battleaxe," while not very commonly used except in literature, are still intelligible to contemporary readers and rightly seen as insulting in intent.

A few remarks about our short list are in order. First, a brief review will reveal that most of these terms fall into one of three categories: animal words, representation of women as playthings or objects to be consumed, and sexual references. Second, some of these terms ("hussy," for instance—like "madam," incidentally) were originally not demeaning but became so; and others became applicable to females exclusively only rather recently. Third, like many (most?) terms we have seen, terms such as "honey," "babe," "doll," and "sweetie-pie" are almost as frequently, if not more frequently, used endearingly. And last, some of these terms have been "rehabilitated," redefined as "positive" terms and not terms of abuse—"bitch," for instance, which we will look at again later. "Slut" seems also to be in rehab. We hear Nate Dogg, in a duet with the rapper Eminem, announce his hunt for "a big old slut" (in the single, "Shake That"); and I read that there is a new lip balm being marketed to young women called Floozy Fruit, Slut Lip Balm.

As for terms of abuse directed at males, such as "oaf," "lunk," "lummox," "bozo," "slob," "goof," "pig," "prick," "jagoff," and the like, it might be noted that the list is probably not as long as the terms for females. Terms such as these, moreover, tend to focus on crudeness and clumsiness, when they are not about sexual activity. In this connection, it should also be noted that some of the most abusive language involves actual or alleged homosexual characteristics. And in that connection, we observe that the same "rehabilitation" as that of "bitch" and "slut" has been in the works for "queer," as we now have academic departments of Queer Studies and the critical school of Queer Criticism. And there is of course "Gay Liberation" and "Gay Pride."

When it comes to sheer numbers, however, slurs on ethnicity and nationality seem over the centuries to have topped the charts. "Barbarian," of course, goes back to ancient Greece, with "heathen" and "infidel" coming soon after without specifically theological connotations. "Savage," too, is what "other peoples" are, when they are not referred to disparagingly by their colonial masters as the "natives." Indeed, "foreigner" can be a term of abuse, and still is in Britain and the United States. (I am reminded of a barman in Cornwall who confessed, "I always wanted to speak a foreign language; and so I went to France and spoke English.") Interestingly, many derogatory terms of this kind have, themselves, "foreign" origins. "Coolie," once used commonly to refer to Chinese (as early, in fact, as the sixteenth century), comes from the Tamil *kuli*, meaning "hireling," for instance; and "Sambo" seems to have originated in Latin America as a term for a mixed-race person with an extremely dark complexion. The list of terms for "foreign" nationals is almost endless. "Turk" and "Greek" alike are recorded as slurs in English (as is "Armenian" by Greeks, even in English). But consider also "bogtrotter" (of the Irish, as early as 1650) and "Mick" or "Paddy"; "dago," "wop," "Eyetie," and "ghinney" (of Italians); "greaseball," "G-boy," or "asshole bandit" (of Greeks); "wetback," "beaner," "spic," "Porky" (of Puerto Ricans); "limey," "anglo," "krauthead," "kraut," "Jerry," "Hun," "Fritz," "polack," "Lugan" (Lithuanian), "bohunk," "honky," "hunky," "dyno" (a Slav, but generically a pick-and-shovel laborer), "Yugo," "herring choker" (of Scandinavians), "Chink," "gook," "Nip," "slope," "Flip" (Filipino), "Wog," "Paki," "camel jockey," "towel-head," "pom" or "pommy" (among Australians, of "Brits"), "sheeny," "yid," "hebe," "kike," and the like. "Frog" is of course a nickname for the French, but it is recorded in English as being used of the Dutch (1652) and even earlier (in 1626) of Jesuits (probably because they were seen as French spies)! One might add that some of these are seldom heard anymore, like "Hun" or "Nip" or even "Jerry," products of wars long past. But they still make the gorge rise in some places. (I have found the remarks of Geoffrey Hughes very helpful, in his *Swearing: A Social History of Foul Language, Oaths and Profanity in English* [Oxford, 1991]).

Some years ago, I ran across a survey published in some journal of urban sociology that was based on questionnaires distributed to persons of varying national and economic classes in different neighborhoods in Chicago (which, at the time, was rather rigidly defined ethnically, religiously, and economically by neighborhood). Respondents were asked to write down all the ethnic slurs they could think of, by ethnic category (see the preceding paragraph for examples). The respondent who wrote down the fewest was a white, middle-class housewife on the fringes of the city; the one who recorded the most was a lieutenant in the Chicago Police Department. Hardly anyone was able to come up with slurs directed at Canadians or Scandinavians (there was not a single entry for Norwegians). Close to the top of the list were anti-Jewish epithets. But by far the greatest number—and this came to no one's surprise—had reference to "Negroes." And the respondent who recorded the largest number of these, I might add, was the police lieutenant.

I cannot reproduce the list that was published, and I will not restrict the following list to African Americans in particular, for many terms of racial abuse are used of blacks in Britain and Canada (and Greater Europe), and not just of blacks who happen to be American. But here are some terms that come to mind without much reflection: "nigger" (or its variants, e.g., "nigrah"), "jig," "jigaboo," "spook," "darkie," "coon," "boogie," "burrhead," "buffalo," "shine," "jungle bunny," "spear-chucker," "swamp guinea," "nightfighter," "spade," "dinge," "eight-ball," "melanzana" (Italian for "eggplant," usually pronounced "melon-john"), "sambo," "buck" (of a male), "brown sugar" (of a female); and then there are terms, largely restricted to Britain and its former colonies, such as "kaffir" or "wog."

I will have more to say about this particular class of terms shortly. But let us look first at some of the patterns that can be detected in the ethnic slurs we have been looking at. With regard to the collection of xenophobic terms ("Turk," "Yugo," "savage," and the others), we find a few that concern physical appearance ("greaseball," "towelhead") and only one referring to imputed sexual deviance ("asshole bandit"). The others are almost all imputations of some primitive cultural practice ("bogtrotter," "camel jockey," and perhaps "beaner"), roughly synonymous with "stupid" ("dyno," "bohunk," "polack," and most of the others that play on the name of the country of origin), or emphases on "otherness" of a more insidious sort ("Hun," "gook," "slope"). What all of them are meant to do, in one way or another, is to belittle the group to which the "other" belongs (or is purported to belong). The terms referring to black people exhibit a pattern that is slightly different, but obviously similar with regard to the objective of denigrating. There are some animal terms ("coon," "buffalo," "bunny," and perhaps "buck"), but there are more terms that refer to physical appearance ("darkie," "shine," "burrhead," "eight-ball") and to cultural practices ("spear-chucker," "jungle bunny," "swamp guinea"). Only two ("buck" and "brown sugar") have any remotely sexual reference. But here again we can easily see that the primary intent behind use of such terms is to belittle. All of them—indeed all that we have considered so far—come down to an arrogation of superiority of the one using them to the one against whom they are used, who are implicitly identified as belonging to an inferior class of beings.

Now we must bear in mind that most of these terms can be used ironically or even as terms not of abuse but of endearment—depending, of course, on the situation or scenario. But we saw before an example of how a term that is normally a term of abuse, "slut," has undergone a rehabilitation of sorts. A similar rehabilitation appears to be taking place with what is perhaps the ethnic slur par excellence, "nigger." Randall Kennedy, a Harvard professor of law, has recently argued for, if not an outright rehabilitation of "nigger," at least a "detoxification" of the term, questioning whether it rightly belongs in the category of "hate speech." In his book (*Nigger: The Strange Career of a Troublesome Word* [New York, 2002]), he points out, correctly, that "nigger" is not uncommonly used in the African American community as a term of familiarity or even of endearment. And he points out (also correctly) that it is in usage in discourse that reaches far beyond the African American community proper—in rap music, for instance, which is commonly listened to by American young people regardless of their race—and indeed has an audience in places like Poland and Spain, as well. So common has it become that it can hardly be bound anymore by the taboos of old. Kennedy, incidentally, was asked to testify for the defense in the trial of a young man of Italian lineage. The young man, from the Howard Beach neighborhood of New York City, was on trial for aggravated assault, but prosecuted for committing a hate crime as well, as witnesses testified that, while beating a young black man with a baseball bat, he repeatedly called his victim "nigger." The defendant was an avid admirer, his attorney argued, of rap music, more specifically, of the rap music of Eminem, a white performer whose use of the term was so casual as to suggest that it was not meant as a term of abuse but of jocular familiarity, what one "brother" called another. In the end, the jury voted for acquittal on the assault charge, but decided that the defendant's use of the bat to rob the victim of various pieces of clothing did qualify as a hate crime, and this meant a sentence of fifteen years in prison. So clearly they did not agree with the argument that "nigger" in this case had been shown to be any less toxic than it had been in the recent past. As the judge put it during the sentencing hearing, the defendant "repeatedly used the 'n' word in ways and in a manner that can best be described as an affront to [the victim's] worth as a human being" (*New York Times*, July 18, 2006).

We will have some observations to make on rap music and related matters in due course. For the present, it might be pointed out that the attempt to show that "nigger" is no longer a term meant to belittle—or at least was not in the case at hand—was not successful. And it is unlikely that it will soon (if ever) be understood as eulogistic—less likely, in any event, than "slut," for example. By contrast, the popularization of the "Black is Beautiful" theme some decades ago did succeed in some measure in attenuating the connotations of inferiority that attached, and in many places still attach, to "black." In both cases, we can see efforts to invert the usual assumptions about what is superior to what by drawing attention to the fact that no term is *inherently* abusive or belittling.

Nonverbal "Terms"

Gestures constitute a considerable part of the "vocabulary" of abuse. Like verbal vehicles, gestures are symbolic actions designated as expressions of put-downs, affront, and ridicule. There is an enormous literature on gesture (going back as far as book 11 of Quintilian's *Institutes*) coming out of fields such as anthropology, social psychology, interpersonal communication—and indeed linguistics, as that field has been assimilated to the more general study of sign systems, or semiotics. Here we can only offer a brief set of observations meant mainly to serve as reminders of the factors of situation and intensity we talked about earlier.

We often associate "gestures" with rather animated use of the hands or other parts of the body to convey an impression or message. But sometimes doing nothing counts as a gesture. A participant in a sit-down strike for instance, or someone remaining immobile on an escalator to prevent anyone else from going up or down, are clearly using gestures (although the latter may be unintentional), even if nothing is "done." *Not* eating a dish placed before you by your host can likewise be seen as a gesture. All of these, after all, are symbolic actions, even if there is no actual "action."

In other instances, the "doing" is quite minimal. Closing one's eyes while someone is remonstrating with you can be seen as a rude gesture. The icy stare of a maître d', playing with one's food, drinking from the wrong glass, putting one's elbows on the table—all of these can be seen as meaningful gestures.

The important word in our examples is, of course, "can," since often people do things for no particular, or at least apparent, reason. Early in Nabokov's *Lolita*, for instance, just after his wife has left him to take up with a Russian taxi driver, Humbert reports,

> I stomped to the bathroom to check if they had taken my English toi-
> let water; they had not; but I noticed with a spasm of fierce disgust
> that the former Counselor of the Tsar, after thoroughly easing his
> bladder, had not flushed the toilet. That solemn pool of alien urine
> with a soggy, tawny cigarette butt disintegrating in it struck me as
> a crowning insult, and I wildly looked around for a weapon. Actu-
> ally I daresay it was nothing but middle-class Russian courtesy (with
> an oriental tang, perhaps) that prompted the good colonel (Maximo-
> vich! His name suddenly taxies back to me), a very formal person as
> they all are, to muffle his private need in decorous silence so as not
> to underscore the small size of his host's domicile with the rush of a
> gross cascade on top of his own hushed trickle. But this did not enter
> my mind at the moment. (30)

On the other side, however, are gestures whose intent is often pain-fully obvious. The one that probably comes to mind most immediately is "giving the finger," or "flipping the bird." Extending one's middle finger in someone's direction is an ancient and perhaps far too com-mon way of expressing one's disdain for another as a nonverbal way of saying "Up yours!" or "Fuck you!" This (the *digitus infamis*), as Tac-itus reports, is the gesture German tribesmen made toward advanc-ing Roman troops; and it is the gesture former vice president Nelson Rockefeller once made to a gathering of anti–Vietnam War protestors. Closely related would be, for instance, the gesture that the Capulets' servant Sampson makes in the first scene of *Romeo and Juliet*: "I will bite my thumb at them [servants of the Montagues], which is a disgrace to them, if they bear it" (1.1.49–50). They do not, of course, bear it, and the famous quarrel in the scene ensues. "Biting one's thumb"—actually "snicking the thumbnail on the upper teeth," as one of Shakespeare's editors explains—is not common today in the United States. But some of us will recall a comparable gesture made by Supreme Court justice Antonin Scalia toward an irksome reporter: the "chin flick," brushing the underside of one's chin with the back of one's fingers, meaning "Don't bother me with your stupid questions" or, more brusquely, "Bug off!" (Some fanciful but often intriguing speculations as to the origin of such gestures can be found in Desmond Morris et al., *Gestures: Their Origins and Distribution* [New York, 1979].) Yet another insulting gesture is the French *cocu*, pointing one's index fingers up, next to the ears, and wiggling the fingers up and down, thus calling someone a cuckold (one of the meanings of *cocu*); this is also the meaning of the more common gesture of holding out one's hand with index finger and little finger extended. Finally, there is what the French call the *bras d'honneur*, but which is quite common in European countries more generally, holding one's arm out in a fist and smacking the other hand (or wrist) onto it above the elbow, swinging the fist arm up. In Italy, this gesture is often accompanied by "*Va, f' an culo*" (commonly, "Bafangoo!" "Go fuck yourself!"). (A possible variant of this might be the trademark gesture by Harpo Marx, thrusting the fisted arm behind the knee of the upraised right leg. Silently, of course.)

There are several other gestures, many of which involve more than just the hand, that are almost universally perceived as insulting: spitting, for instance, or baring the buttocks (mooning), which, I am told, is a gesture of rejection even in Kenya and Zimbabwe. There are some gestures, however, that may be signs of approval in the United States, but are insulting in other cultural settings. The "thumbs up" gesture, for instance, is the equivalent of "Up yours!" in Mediterranean and Latin American areas; and the "ring gesture" (touching the tip of the index finger to end of the thumb to form a circle) is a sign of approval ("A-okay") in New York or San Francisco, but an obscene gesture (sometimes with homosexual connotations) in Athens or Istanbul. Like many verbal terms of abuse, in short, gestures can also be insulting, or very insulting, depending on the situation and cultural setting.

Drawing attention to a similarity between gestures and verbal terms will not in itself clarify much about what we might mean in talking about the "language" of insult in such a way as to include both verbal and nonverbal signs. To say that both are "symbolic actions" is not to say anything very illuminating, at least at one level. But when we ask ourselves "symbolic of what?" we begin to see that both gestures and their verbal counterparts must both be read in the context of the dimensions and social dynamics we talked about at the outset of our reflections on insults. But there may be more. It is interesting to note that, in their attempts to explain the origins of various gestures (and thereby, in anthropological fashion, to explain why they mean what they do), Morris and his colleagues often drift into rhetorical territory. "Giving the finger" is, as it turns out, a visual metaphor for sexual prowess; and the "ring gesture," in certain situations, one for sexual deviance. The "chin flick," they tell us (170–71), is a symbolic way of asserting one's masculinity—or another's lack of it. It is no accident that the French name for this gesture is *la barbe*, "the beard"; and a similar case might be made for the origin and significance of the *bras d'honneur*. And speaking of beards and arms, are we not in the realm of a sort of rhetorical synecdoche? And what of the use of a gesture to "cap" an accumulation of verbal terms of abuse, as in the "And I speak as a friend" that we saw earlier? I do not mean to push this too far. But it may serve to remind us that, in discussing a rhetoric of insult, we must not be too quick to make of "verbal" and "nonverbal" separate matters of consideration. After all, the traditional rhetorics summed up in Quintilian, for instance, would never dream of a speech given, or even conceived, without "nonverbal" accompaniment.

The Problem of the Intrinsic

So far, we have seen that there is a measure of indeterminacy in both words and gestures—that is, that there appear to be no inherently abusive terms, but that it all depends on scenario, or situation: who is saying what to whom, and why either of them should care. But there are some gestures and words that seem to have no other function than to belittle or scorn or put down—the *bras d'honneur*, for instance, or a word like "nigger" or "cunt." So perhaps instead of stating flatly that there are no inherently abusive terms, we should say that, for some terms, it is exceedingly difficult to imagine a scenario in which they are *not* abusive. Yet if there are no terms that are inherently abusive, there seem to be some qualities or aspects of individuals or groups that are always subjects for abuse. Physical appearance, for instance, whether regarding body parts or attire, is everywhere, it seems, the subject of insults. Family ties, particularly relations with siblings or parents, are likewise universally vulnerable—especially in regard to allegations of incestuous relationships or illegitimacy. Of course, the question might be asked, What *else* would you insult? What is important, however, is not the vocabulary of body parts or familial relations, but the equation of those parts or relations with a more generalized "otherness." In other words, it is not the terms but the insinuations that count.

Taking up body parts, then, what about "cunt"? Is calling someone "cunt" always a way of insulting that person? While it may be difficult to imagine a situation where it is not, we know that in Chaucer, for instance, "cunt," or the Middle English version, "queynte," is not always a term of abuse—in fact, its attested usage is quite different. In "The Miller's Tale" (A3276, 94; references are to *The Complete Works of Geoffrey Chaucer*, vol. 4, ed. Walter W. Skeat [Oxford, 1958]), for instance, we read, "And prively he caught hir by the queynte," where it is simply a name for the part. In the prologue to "The Wife of Bath's Tale," the word means a bit more: at A332 (330), she says, "Ye shul have queynte right y-nough at eve" and, a little later (A444, 333), "Is it for ye wold have my queynte alone?"—by which she seems to mean what she calls three lines later a "*bele chose*," with particular reference to the joys of sex (see D608, 337). Of course, that was Chaucer—long ago. But in the far more recent *Lady Chatterley's Lover* (ed. Michael Squires [Cambridge, 1993]), we find the gamekeeper Mellors saying to the significantly named Connie, "Tha'rt good cunt, though, aren't ter? Best bit o'cunt left on earth. When ter likes! When tha'rt willin'! . . . Cunt! Eh, that's the beauty o'thee, lass!" (177–78). And Connie, far from being insulted or offended, is aroused and seduced.

Connie may not have been offended, but some important critics were—notably Raymond Mortimer, in whose January 1929 *Dial* review the book is called "a hymn of hate against the intellect." But if there was any objection to "cunt," it was an objection to its obscenity; and that brings up a point that ought to be made here: that just as not all insults or terms of abuse are obscene, not all obscene terms are terms of abuse.

In other cases, what might be regarded as both obscene and insulting is a term like "mother fucker," which, with its intimations of incest, might qualify as an ultimate insult. But even there, we find that the term is often used (like "nigger," and not just by Kennedy's account) without either obscene or insulting intent. It is not unusual, in some parts, to hear, "Hey, you old mother fucker! How you doin'?" clearly without reference to actual mothers or to some vulgar sex act. The key word here is, of course, "intent"; for no term, obscene or not, can be considered an insult unless it is intended to be an insult. (This is not to deny that some people are "insulted" when they shouldn't be; but that is a different matter.)

If "intent" is the key word, we may be approaching some deep and murky waters. But we needn't address such old philosophical chestnuts such as "Can we know other minds?" There are several more concrete and particular questions we can ask of a suspected insult that can help us sort things out. Obviously, the first question is whether there is an expressed intention to insult. But how likely is it that anyone would preface an insult with "I'm going to insult you now"? That's not only tactically unwise (forewarned is forearmed), but also perhaps inelegant. On the other hand, what tone can we pick up? Any contempt? Sarcasm? Of course, it's hard to pick such things up when dealing with a written document—but it's clearly not impossible. Further, what is your relation to someone you suspect has just insulted you? Or, backing this question up a little, what makes you suspect that? Have there been previous instances in which intent was evident? Is the suspected insulter a "known offender" with a reputation for being insulting? Is there a grain of truth in what the insulter says—and does there need to be such a grain of truth? In any event, what grain of truth is there in a gesture—in Humbert's toilet bowl, for instance? Does the suspected insult replicate or resemble other utterances or gestures you know with some certainty have counted as insults—i.e., is the suspected insult consistent with other, conventionally recognized insults? As we shall see in the next chapter, there is a stock of insult commonplaces that, while hardly universal, cover a mighty broad range of what we might regard as "insult literature." At the same time, we might ask ourselves if it is possible to imagine a scenario in which a term of abuse (or some statement built around it) is actually not insulting and should not be taken as such? See the comments earlier on "Hey, you old mother fucker!"

Questions like these are at the heart of what educators these days call "critical thinking." And they resemble, for instance, the rules that the old rhetoricians laid down for dealing with ambiguity in a written document, or the issues to be explored (the inventories of *circumstantiae* or *peristaseis* we find in the old rhetorical handbooks) in the process of inventing an argument. This is no coincidence, since they are all, actually, questions that properly belong to rhetoric. And, of course, what we are aiming for here is a rhetoric of insults. They are also, it might be added, the sorts of questions that come into play in everyday social interactions. We don't of course (or don't often) explicitly ask them; but it is our answers to just such questions that help us size up social situations in general.

In that connection, there are two particular kinds of social interaction that share a great deal with insult: jokes and irony. Like insults, they invite us to ask not what is the relation between what is said and what is meant, but who "means" it, and where and when?—i.e., rhetorical questions, not philological or grammatical questions. So, in reference to jokes, it is said, "You had to be there." And the reason for this is that, as Ted Cohen observes in his book on jokes (*Jokes* [Chicago, 1999], appropriately enough), telling jokes is a social transaction that is successful only when the teller and the listener are in possession of a shared background, and can bring this to the joke. Likewise, I will argue, with insults. And as for irony, here is what Wayne Booth wrote thirty-odd years ago:

> Irony, when perceived and appreciated, completes a more astonishing communal achievement than most accounts have recognized. Its complexities are, after all, shared: the whole thing cannot work unless both parties to the exchange have confidence that they are moving together in identical patterns . . . [E]ven the most simple-minded irony, when it succeeds, reveals in both participants a kind of meeting with other minds that contradicts a great deal that gets said about who we are and whether we can know each other. (*Rhetoric of Irony*, 13)

Appreciating insults as comparable to jokes and irony does not, of course, provide us with "a sure way," by any means. In his book, Booth reports reading a student paper describing in great and vivid detail the killing and butchering of a deer. As an inveterate nonhunter and a man not given to killing of any sort, he took the student's paper to be a masterpiece in the tradition of Swift's "A Modest Proposal." He gave the paper high marks. But the student told him that, no, it wasn't at all meant as irony. He really was a devoted hunter who thought it important to explain in detail how to dress a deer properly out in the woods. What Booth then realized was that he had not really understood the paper, but not because he didn't understand the words in it. He was simply in another "moral universe." Likewise, as I hope some of my examples will show, not realizing when one has been insulted or that one is being insulting is the result of living in different moral universes. And as Booth understood, once that other moral universe is revealed, social faux pas resulting from perceived, but unintended, insults can be atoned for. So it becomes clear that the important questions are not semantic or epistemological but questions of how to maintain good human relations. And there is no "sure way" of doing that.

In the course of the preceding introductory—and, because of that, superficial—observations, I have tried to sketch out the dimensions and, at somewhat greater length, the particular vehicles of insult, largely verbal but not limited to words. The examples I have provided—ones I hope are readily recognizable as insults of various sorts—are in some cases drawn from documented sources and in other cases made up. But all of them have been brief.

These brief examples were meant to provide some clues as to what to look for and what to pay attention to in examining this interesting and important aspect of human relations—understood, obviously, as capable of being both adversarial and cooperative. But it is time now to get serious about our "inductive" procedure and look closely at some more extended examples—all of them, I hasten to add, real (although in many cases literary) and not invented for this volume.

Accordingly, I will in the next section examine at some length examples of discourse that is obviously intended to insult, either because the speakers in question tell us explicitly that they intend their words to be insulting or because the very setting of their discourse defines it as insulting. The examples I have chosen are drawn from a wide range of sources and traditions. They serve on one side to illustrate the variety and richness of insult-in-action; but I hope they will also help us to uncover in a systematic fashion some principles that might serve in turn to illuminate what holds that variety together and that will help us not only to interpret what we see but to appreciate as well the inventive genius and artistic calculation that masters of insult bring to their tasks.

CHAPTER 2

Traditional Principles of Insult

In this section, I want to draw attention to some fundamental aspects of insult that are overlooked or, I think, misconstrued by the sociological, anthropological, philological, and philosophical perspectives. As a friend of mine once put it, it is not so much that they have looked through the wrong end of the telescope; they have the wrong telescope. In the examples that follow—certainly not random, and rather more extended than the ones we have already looked at—I hope to tease out the principles of a rhetoric of insult as they operate, as it were, "in action."

Sex, Lies, and Rhetorical Community

It might be said that the last decades of the Roman republic, from about 63 to 43 BCE, were the heyday of invective, a period of unprecedented vitriol and nastiness in public discourse that historians over the last centuries have found so distasteful as to throw into question the so-called glorious history of Rome. That judgment might be the result, at least in part, of the nature of the sources historians have had to deal with. Documentation of what happened more than two thousand years ago is bound to be, at the very least, sketchy; and what has survived has no doubt been tainted by generations of selection, suppression, and simple loss due to the corruptibility of the materials used to save the records of what transpired during those years. It is also a coincidence—or perhaps it is not a coincidence—that a great deal of the evidence historians look to comes from the literary output of one man, Cicero, from precisely the same decades; and surely one cannot expect a man who made his fortunes as a lawyer and a politician to be entirely trustworthy. But however much one might view Cicero's accounts of the events between 63 and 43 BCE with suspicion, one fact remains incontestable: he was a master of insult.

The invective at which Cicero was so skilled may be a reflection of the state of Roman politics at the time. We are not concerned here to set the record straight or to dredge up any hitherto unexamined evidence, but it might be useful to provide a little background. The most generous phrase to sum the political matter up would be "gang warfare." A chronicle of the last decades of the republic would trace a succession of alignments and realignments among the rich and powerful—among whom would be numbered the likes of Julius Caesar, Mark Antony, and, of course, Cicero himself—in order to exert the maximum of influence and profit; this involved a parallel succession of such things as enforced exile, confiscation of property, and assassinations. Rome, one might say, was a city of Mean Streets.

Another tactic in this milieu that seems to have been common was calumny, using public communication to destroy the reputation and standing of an opponent, and one means of doing that was making allegations of sexual misconduct or deviance. For example, in the second of his speeches against Catiline in 63, Cicero sets himself up as the spokesman for traditional Roman values and Catiline, accused of fomenting a coup d'état, as subverting those values. What kind of man, he says, would surround himself with "men whom I see flitting about in the Forum . . . glistening with unguents and resplendent in purple"? (5 [references to Cicero are to section numbers]); who had brought with him on campaign a person "with whom he had had an affair while he was only a lad"? (4). "Who ever was as active a seducer of the young as he? With some, he took his pleasure most disgustingly [*turpissime*], with others he pandered to their shameful desires [*amori flagitiosissime serviebat*], to others he offered reward for their obscene desires [*fructum libidinum*]" (10). Later in the speech, he again paints a sordid picture of Catiline's associates, his bosom friends: "These are the ones you see with their pompadours, dripping with oil, some as smooth as young girls . . . wearing frocks, not togas." They are all adulterers and filthy minded lechers (*impuri impudicique*), "dainty and effeminate boys who have learned not only to dance and sing, but also to brandish knives and sprinkle about poisons"; "an elite retinue of little whores [*cohortem scortorum*]" (23–24). That is not all, of course. Not only are Catiline and his friends lechers and deviants, they are gluttons and drunks (10, in a particularly vivid passage), spend-thrifts (4, 10, 18), embezzlers and bribetakers (7, 18, 19, 21), and aspiring tyrants (1, 19).

Only with this last charge does Cicero come close to relevance to the charges against Catiline, which he had covered in his earlier speech and to which he returns at the end of this one, where he speaks in his capacity as consul, or chief executive. But the greater part of the speech is, basically, character assassination on grounds that have little to do with Catiline's political aspirations.

For promoting Catiline's political aspirations, Catiline's coconspirators were executed, on Cicero's order and without trial. In the aftermath, Cicero himself was later found to have acted illegally and was forced into exile in the farther reaches of Northern Greece. This seems to have resulted in, among other things, the end of his friendship with another prominent Roman politician, L. Calpurnius Piso. Piso became consul in 58, enjoying the patronage of the powerful triumvirate of Pompey, L. Crassus, and Julius Caesar, who married Piso's daughter, Calpurnia, in 59. On his return from exile, Cicero himself competed for a place in Rome under the triumvirate, and soon came into conflict with Caesar and with his old friend Piso. In 55, Cicero delivered—and had published—a speech attacking Piso.

In this speech, Cicero makes no case for "blameworthy by association," as he had in the *Second Catilinarian*, but attacks Piso personally, and with brio. Piso, Cicero asserts, is at base a lowlife from a disreputable family (despite his pretensions):

> There is something broken-down, groveling, abject, sordid, and mean about you, even lower than would seem to befit your grandfather, the auctioneer of Milan (62).

(And see, e.g., 53, 67, and 87.) This may be inferred from his very appearance: bad teeth, hairy cheeks, and unusual dress (as we gather from the fragmentary opening of the speech). He is also a thief (e.g., 24, 38, 66) and a bribetaker (83–84, 87); and he cultivates a following of flatterers (22, 67, 70). But more than that, he is a drunk and a lecher:

> You would never have plunged yourself in such shameful disgrace [*flagitia*], but you listen to them [Greek "philosophers"] in your taverns and brothels [see *stupris*] over food and wine (42);

[Piso] lolled about in the stink and drink of his Greek companions . . .
No one can say whether he spent more time drinking or throwing up
or pissing (22);

. . . Greeks packed five deep or more on a couch, himself alone on one,
toping until the wine is poured straight from the jug (67).

(And see 13, 66–67, 72, 83, etc.) What is particularly striking is the use
to which Cicero puts the *lexicon invectivae*: Piso is a beast (*belua*, 1, 8),
a servile beast (*pecus*, 19), a dog (*canis*, 23), a vulture (*voltorius*, 38), an
ass (*asinus*, 73), and a "sex-mechanic" (*admissarius*, lit., "stallion," 69).
He is a murderer (*carnifex*, 11, 18, 30), a plague and a scoundrel (*pestis*,
scelus, 3, 56), a gallows-bird (*furcifer*, 14), an enemy and traitor (*hostis*,
proditor, 24, 78), and a bandit (*gladiator* at 18 and 28). He is, in short, a
turd (*lutulentus* at 1 and 27, *caenum* at 13, *sordes* at 62).

A little more than a decade after the speech against Piso, in late autumn
of 44, Cicero published (as a pamphlet) a "speech" against Mark Antony, the second of a series of orations that Cicero conceived as his *Philippics*, after the speeches against Philip II of Macedon (Alexander the
Great's father) by Demosthenes in Athens in the fourth century BCE.
Second Philippic was composed as a speech delivered before the Roman
Senate (it was not), with Antony present (he was not), and it exhibits
the same genius for insult as the other two we have just seen. Unlike
Antony's fictional presence in the audience of this oration, the events
referred to in it are not fictional (though they are sometimes distorted),
and Antony truly had emerged as one of the most powerful politicians
in Rome after the assassination of Julius Caesar. This Cicero saw as a
mortal threat to the continued existence of the republic.

Cicero's attack against Antony is deeply personal, as was, evidently,
a speech Antony had delivered attacking Cicero. Accordingly, we find,
as we might have expected, nasty references to Antony's family background (2, 69) and odd attire (76–77); and we hear Antony called "a
gladiator," meaning that he was little better than a slave given the job
of maiming or killing another for the entertainment of the crowd—a
conventional insult in Roman political oratory. But two far more frequent charges against Antony are his "audacity and impudence" (*au-
dacia, impudentia*: see 1, 4, 9, 16, 23, 43ff., 61, etc.); and his "stupidity"

(*stultitia*: see, e.g., 8–9, 23, 29, 42, 80–81, 97, etc.). And these, in turn, are connected with Antony's chief character defect, his depravity.

The litany of Antony's depraved acts is very long indeed. He is accused of being a careless gambler (104), a coward (71), and a thief (62, 93). But more, he is (as Piso was, by Cicero's account) a drunk and a lecher; and Cicero goes into minute, and sometimes scandalous, detail to support those charges. He sets our expectations right at the beginning of the speech, at 3:

> You have brought this up, I suppose, to commend yourself to the dregs of society [*infimo ordine*], since everyone would remember that you had been the son-in-law of a freed slave [*libertinus*] and your children had been grandsons of Quintus Fadius, another freed slave . . . You said you withdrew your candidacy for the augurate in my favor. What incredible audacity [*incredibilem audaciam*]! What crying impudence! At the time, I was the candidate favored by the College of Augurs . . . you were bankrupt [*nec solvendo*], nor did you think you could save yourself unless there was a revolution—or so you thought.

A little later (at the end of 43), Cicero launches into an account of Antony's shabby history. After reminding his audience of Antony's bankruptcy, he describes his search for "patronage":

> You came of age, and at once turned your man's toga in for a woman's [*mulier*]. You were right then a common whore [*volgare scortum*]. You set your price for the disgusting deed [*flagiti*], and it was a high one. But Curio soon turned up; and he took you off the streets [*a meretricio quaestu*], and set you up in a matron's gown as if he had arranged a real marriage for you. No slave-boy bought for sex [*emptus libidinis*] was ever so much in his master's power as you were in Curio's. (43–44)

Just how corrupt was Antony is beyond words (see *non possum dicere* at the beginning of 47)—but before long, Cicero has found some:

> Let us take up the most depraved sort of irresponsibility [*de nequissimo genere levitatis*] . . . You had swilled down so much wine at the wedding of Hippias that you had to vomit it all up the next day right before the eyes of the Roman people. What a disgusting performance, even to hear about, much less to see! . . . In a gathering of Roman peo-

ple doing public business . . . where a belch would be disgusting [*turpe esset*], he [Antony] threw up and filled his own lap—and the entire dais!—with gobbets of food reeking of wine! (63)

Cicero describes what Antony and his fellow revelers did to Pompey's estate after having it confiscated:

Whole storerooms were lavished on utter ne'er-do-wells. "Actors" looted a number of things, actresses some others. The house was crammed with gamblers, swarmed with drunks, drinking went on for days on end. (67)

And in the closing parts of Cicero's account, at 104:

For how many days were you carousing [*perbacchantis*] in that [another] villa! The drinking began in mid-morning, then the gaming, then the vomiting. Poor house! . . . [105] every part of the building echoed with drunken shouting, the mosaic floors were awash in wine, the walls dripped with it; boys of good families were found among the catamites [*cum meritoriis*] and whores among mothers of families.

So Antony's drunkenness and lechery are charges that Cicero spends a fair amount of time describing and amplifying. Notably missing, however, are the traditional terms of abuse we saw in the other speeches, and there are very few metaphoric versions of those terms. Cicero seems to want to narrate (his version of) the concrete details of Antony's unspeakable actions, not to cast them in terms of, say, animal comparisons. And, of course, it is not his drinking and whoring that are the real problems, for they are simply manifestations of Antony's essential flaws: audacity (see, e.g., 1, 4, 9, 15 [*impudentia*], 42, 43, 44, 46, 65, 68, 70, 83, etc.) and stupidity (8 [*stultitia*], 9 [*amentia*], 23, 29, 42, 65, 80, 97, etc.). We will look again at such charges later.

If Cicero's speech was meant originally as a response to Antony's, it served well as a damning portrait of his adversary that would stay in the back of his audience's mind during the course of the continued attacks Cicero launched over the next months—there are, all together, fourteen *Philippics*. It certainly stayed in Antony's mind, as before the next year was over, he arranged to have Cicero eliminated from Rome's political scene. While he was on his way to the port of Caieta to make his escape to Greece, Cicero was assassinated. After they had slain him, his murderers brought his head to Antony, who ordered it to be displayed in the forum. Then, the historian Dio tells us (his account can be found in book 47.8.3ff.), Fulvia, the wife of Antony's ally Octavian, got hold of it,

> took the head in her hands . . . and after abusing it and spitting on it out of spite, set it on her knees and opened the mouth, and pulled out the tongue, and pierced it with hairpins while muttering brutal insults over it.

But let us get back to our speeches. What we see is only a tiny sample of the role played by insult, particularly sexual allegations, in Cicero's political oratory—and, presumably, in others' oratory of the time as well. But there is enough in what we have seen to begin drawing some conclusions. First, all of them touch on a similar set of topics for abuse, though with varying emphases. Gluttony and drunkenness, aberrant sexual behavior, the plundering of public funds, and the taking of bribes appear as themes in all three. We find attention also paid to family origins and physical appearances. Bankruptcy or the squandering of family wealth also appear as topics of abuse. The present selection is, of course, very limited—and, one might say, very selective; but the topics are representative of those touched upon in a great many of Cicero's speeches, both political and courtroom speeches. In fact, so common are such topics that many scholars are beginning to suspect that they were, in fact, stock topics, i.e., commonplaces, a list of which, like the commonplaces concerning persons and deeds that Cicero inventories in his rhetorical treatises, could be consulted and drawn upon in the process of rhetorical invention. Indeed, they are common not only in Cicero, but go back to the rhetorical practices of the Greeks four hundred years before Cicero's time.

Here, in any case, are the stock topics of Roman invective:

1. Embarrassing family origin
2. Unworthy of one's family
3. Physical appearance
4. Eccentricity of dress
5. Gluttony and drunkenness
6. Hypocrisy for appearing virtuous

7. Greed and prodigality
8. Taking bribes
9. Pretentiousness
10. Unacceptable sexual conduct
11. Hostility to family
12. Cowardice in battle
13. Aspiring to tyranny
14. Bankruptcy or other financial embarrassment
15. Cruelty to fellow citizens or allies
16. Plunder of private or public property
17. Oratorical ineptitude

To this list, we might add, in view of *Second Philippic*,

18. Stupidity

(There is a useful discussion of these in R. G. M. Nisbet's edition of Cicero's *In Pisonem* [Oxford, 1961], 192–97.) Of course, not all of these are equally "common." What the list represents is an inventory of available topics that, as Cicero tells "Cicero Junior" in the *Partitions of Oratory*, a speaker should review to find available material for the arguments at hand. Not all are, obviously, equally applicable in every case— "cowardice in battle" or "oratorical ineptitude," for instance. Nevertheless, a review of speeches in which invective plays an important part usually turns up several, if not most, of these topics.

The topics are "common," then, in the sense that they appear with relative frequency in oratorical performances. They are also "common" in that they are not limited in their application to a particular individual, but may apply in a variety of cases. For example, in 99 of the *Second Philippic*, Cicero complains that Antony had unjustifiably maligned Dolabella, alleging adultery:

> you are so bold [*ausus es*] as to allege this as your reason for hating Dolabella, that you discovered that he attempted adultery with your cousin and wife. Who can assess whether you were more impudent [*impudentior*] to speak like that in the Senate, or more reckless to do so against Dolabella, or more lacking in decency as to say it while your uncle was in the audience, or more cruel as to make that allegation against that unhappy woman in such a foul and evil fashion?

Some months later, however, after Dolabella changes his allegiance and goes over to Antony's side, Cicero makes a similar charge against Dolabella (see *Eleventh Philippic* 9), using almost the exact same language he had used in *Second Philippic* 47 against Antony!

It is cases such as this that make historians suspicious when they see "commonplace" charges leveled against a speaker's opponents, whether the speaker be a Roman or a Greek or, for that matter, an Englishman. Members of a speaker's audience who had heard similar charges before might be just as suspicious. But there is a third sense in which commonplaces are "common" that explains their plausibility: the fact that commonplaces reflect or sum up "what everybody knows." "Everybody knows" that politicians are greedy and corrupt. "Everybody knows" that the powerful and influential attend wild parties and indulge in bizarre sexual behavior (and we should remind ourselves that the members of Cicero's audience were themselves powerful and influential). "Everybody knows" that people who can't speak coherently are either stupid or putting on an act. And so, even in a situation where a given politician is neither, in fact, corrupt nor putting on an act, it *could* be true, it "makes sense," "it could happen."

Cicero is a master at negotiating the incompatibilities between suspicion and plausibility. Explaining in any detail how he does this would take us far afield, so we need to be content here to make a few general observations about the persuasive strategies Cicero deploys. For one thing, he recognizes that his audience—powerful and influential and used to hearing invective as its members were—is like the jaded lady who says to her chef, "*Étonnez moi!*" That is, they expect to hear tales about greed and corruption, but they expect to hear something "new," or at least put in a forceful and engaging and novel way— forceful enough to allow the plausibility to prevail over the suspicion. These collective expectations Cicero both shapes and fulfills, and at several levels at once.

Thus, when we look closely, we can see that it is not mere literary embellishment that he seeks when he calls Piso a *furcifer* or a *pecus* or a *volturius*—all metaphors echoing the terms of abuse of Roman comedy, and directed at devious servants, at that. Even in the construction of his sentences, Cicero shapes and fulfills expectations: climactic sequences in three- and four-part arrangements—repeatedly (e.g., *Second Catili-*

narian 1, 13, 19, 21, etc.)—or in his repetition of "rhetorical questions" (7, 12, etc.) or exclamations (10). And what of his "eye-witness" details: Antony casting aside his man's toga, throwing up in his own lap the "gobbets of food and drink," the riotous party in Pompey's house? Cicero was, clearly, not there; but this is good stuff!

It is not only collective expectations—of everything from topics to sentence structure—that Cicero exploits, however. He also taps into some of the deeper recesses of the social presumptions held by his listeners: the presumption that social rank is significant, that honor can be attained or lost, that the opinions of others are important and one's reputation matters greatly, that there are bonds of intimacy that are crucial yet fragile, that prestige can be measured by one's family ties, good looks, and financial security; that, in short, dignity and status are at the core of both domestic and public life. These are, of course, a different sort of expectation—not just of what is going to happen, but of how one ought to comport oneself, and why it should matter. And finally, we should bear in mind that Cicero's exploitation of his audience's expectations is calculated, arranged, and performed with consummate skill, and not just a matter of intuition or of guile.

All Those Nauseous Epigrams of Martial

This title is from the end of Byron's *Don Juan*, canto 1, stanza 43 (from 1818), after which (in 44 and 45) he goes on to remark on the absurdity of relegating epigrams by Martial deemed obscene to an appendix or special sequestered section in then available editions. Byron expresses hope that someday

> some less rigid editor shall stoop
> To call them back into their separate cages,
> Instead of standing all together,
> Like garden gods—and not so decent either.

I was struck, when I read these lines years ago, by the thought that things hadn't changed much a century and a half (at the time) later. In widely used Loeb Classical Library editions of such poets as Martial, Catullus, and Juvenal, which printed the Latin text on the left-hand page and a rendering into English on the right-hand page, I and my fellow students often found Latin on both sides—a clear signal that those were the truly interesting passages. And so only the good Latinists in my college had access to the "lascivious" parts of those poets that we were not allowed—or at least not encouraged—to read. Happily, this is no longer the case; and as the Loeb editors have decided to "tell it like it is," I feel free here to do the same.

Marcus Valerius Martialis was born, in Spain, about a century after Cicero's death (c. 40–104 CE); migrated, like many of his contemporaries (Quintilian, for one) to Rome; and by gaining the support of influential patrons was able to move in upper-class Roman circles and to become a well-known and widely admired poet. Indeed, he was made an honorary member of the Equestrian Order, and, as such, had opportunity to mingle with members of the senate and, on occasion, with courtiers in the imperial court. In the 80s and 90s his poems were recognized by booksellers in Rome as commercially viable, and he was able to publish twelve carefully constructed booklets (*libelli*) of his epigrams for consumption and appreciation by upper-class readers (Pliny the Younger, for one) in and about Rome.

Not all of his epigrams (short—sometimes not so short—verse compositions so called because originally made up to be engraved on various objects) are obscene. Many of them are generic portraits of the simple life of his country of birth, favorite places, and what poets have to endure. However, many of them, not all of them "nauseous," are quite nasty attacks on various figures of Roman society built around the very loci of invective we looked at in Cicero: "embarrassing family origin," for instance, at book 1.81 ("You know that you are slave-born, Sosibianus, and you blandly / admit it when you call your father 'sir.'"); lowly occupations (3.7, 11.14, 4.86 [fishmongers], or 11.5 and 11.6 [pimps]), ugliness (e.g., 1.10, 2.33, 2.35, 3.39, 3.42, and 3.72, etc.); "eccentricity of dress" (5.23, etc.); "squandering one's patrimony" (9.82); gluttony (3.17, 5.70, 7.20, 8.23, etc.), even "oratorical ineptitude" (8.7, for instance). And, of course, there are scores that have to do with drunkenness (see, e.g., 1.87, 2.73, and 11.70) and aberrant sexual behavior (as in, e.g., 1.34, 1.90, 2.51, etc.). We will examine some of these in due course.

More striking, in the present instance, are some that suggest that Martial had in mind the same Cicero as the one we saw before. For instance, book 3.66 (I have used here Shackleton-Bailey's prose translations, with various revisions):

Antony committed a crime equal to the weapon of Pharos. Both cut off a sacred head. The one, Rome, was yours when you joyfully celebrated laureled triumphs, the other when you spoke. Yet, Antony's case is worse than Pothinus's [who murdered Pompey]: he did the deed for his master, Antony for himself.

Or book 5.69:

Antony, you have no stone to throw at Pharian Pothinus. Cicero makes you more guilty than your [proscription] lists. Why do you in your madness draw a sword against the mouth of Rome? Not even Catiline would have committed this atrocity. An impious soldier is bribed with accursed gold, and for so great a sum you buy the silence of a single voice. What avails the costly stillness of the sacred tongue? All mankind will begin to speak in Cicero's stead.

And see book 11.20, in which Antony comes together with a lubricious Fulvia; or book 2.89, addressed to one Gaurus:

You enjoy stretching the evening with overmuch wine. That I forgive: you have the same bad habit as Cato, Gaurus. You write verses without Apollo and the Muses. For this you deserve praise, for that was Cicero's habit. Your vomiting: a habit of Antony. Your extravagance, of Apicius. But your sucking—whose bad habit is that?

While these may give a general idea of the tone and content one finds in Martial, they do not begin to convey the sorts of things Martial was very good at, and, accordingly, why he became so popular in his own day—much less why he has been recognized as a poet for all ages since the Renaissance. For one thing, translations in general, but especially prose translations, miss, when they do not obscure, a great deal. Martial was an accomplished Latin poet, and so the examples of his invective that follow will be provided in Latin as well as in (prose) translation. Only in this way will we be able to see how his epigrams "work." We can begin with a couple of two-line epigrams from book 1:

80
Sportula, Cane, tibi suprema nocte petita est.
occidit, puto, te, Cane, quod una fuit.

[Canus, you looked for a dinner-present the night you died. I think it killed you, Canus, that there was only one.]

83

Os et labra tibi lingit, Manneia, catellus:
non mirror, merdas si libet esse cani.

[Manneia, your little dog licks your mouth and lips. Small wonder, if a dog likes eating turds.]

If I read these correctly, we are seeing here two examples of epigrammatic insult. A *sportula*, evidently, was a little gift of food or even money given to dinner guests ("clients") by their host (the "patron"), and this came to be the term for any gratuity given by patrons to their clients. In this case, Canus died, the poet says, of disappointment at getting only one—after he had a free dinner—and so it was his greediness and, perhaps, his gluttony that were his downfall—loci nos. 7 and 5 in the list we compiled earlier. The lines addressed to Manneia put the phrase "lap dog" in a new light if we understand "*os et labra*" to refer not to her mouth and lips but to parts of the female genitalia. Such an interpretation would be consistent with Martial's expressed distaste for oral sex—cunnilingus in particular—in several other epigrams. Manneia, then, is being charged with "unacceptable sexual conduct," locus no. 10.

An epigram at book 7.20 exhibits something similar. It is rather longer, but deserves full quotation here:

Nihil est miseries neque gulosius Santra.
rectam vocatus cum cucurrit ad cenam,
quam tot diebus noctibusque captavit,
ter poscit apri glandulas, quater lumbum,
et utramque coxam leporis et duos armos,
nec erubescit peierare de turdo
et ostreorum rapere lividos cirros.
buccis placentae sordidam linit mappam;
illic et uvae collocantur ollares
et Punicorum pauca grana malorum
et excavatae pellis indecens vulvae
et lippa ficus deblisque boletus.

sed mappa cum iam mille rumpitur furtis,
rosos tepenti spondylos sinu condit
et devorato capite turturem truncum.
colligere longa turpe nec putat dextra
analecta quidquid et canes reliquerunt.
nec esculenta sufficit gulae praeda:
mixto lagonam replete ad pedes vino.
haec per ducentas cum domum tulit scalas
seque obserata clusit anxius cella
gulosus ille, postero die vendit.

[Santra is the most miserly and the greediest of beings. When he has an invitation and runs off to a formal dinner, for which he has been angling for so many days and nights, he asks for three helpings of boar's sweetmeats, four of loin, both haunches of hare, and two shoulders; nor does he blush to lie about a thrush and snatch the milky beards of oysters. He smears his dirty napkin with mouthfuls of cake. Therein are assembled preserved grapes and a few pomegranate grains, and the ugly skin of a hollowed matrix and an oozy fig and a crippled mushroom. But when the napkin bursts with a thousand thefts, he hides gnawed vertebrae in his warm pocket together with the remains of a pigeon whose head has been devoured. Nor does he think shame to collect with a long arm whatever the sweeper and the dogs have left. Edible plunder is not enough for his gullet. He fills a flagon at his feet with mixed wine. When he has carried all this home up two hundred stairs and anxiously shut himself in his barred chamber, this greedy fellow—sells it all the next day.]

Gluttony again (no. 5)—and even more stupendous gluttony if we translate "*mappa*" in line 13 as "tablecloth" instead of "napkin"; and "*praeda*" at the end of line 18 shows that Martial is thinking also in terms of no. 16, "plunder of private or public property." And clearly, the catalogue of gourmet dishes and goodies at lines 4–15, along with the "*analecta*" left by the cleaners and dogs, is meant to indicate that Santra has a prodigious case of avarice—see no. 7 in our list of loci. But the real power of the epigram stems not from its *accumulatio* but from its punchline, a classic instance of the device the Ancients called *para prosdokian*—a sudden violation of expectations—that functions as a sort of cap to the whole thing.

Another cluster of loci can be seen in book 9.27:

Cum depilatos, Chreste, coleos portes
et vulturino mentulam parem collo
et prostitutis levius caput culis,
nec vivat ullus in tuo pilus crure
purgentque saevae cana labra vulsellae;
Curios, Camillos, Quintios, Numas, Ancos,
et quidquid usquam legimus pilosorum
loqueris sonasque grandibus minax verbis,
et cum theatris saeculoque rixaris.
occurrit aliquis inter ista si draucus,
iam paedagogo liberatus et cuius
refibulavit turgidum faber penem,
nutu vocatum ducis, et pudet fari
Catoniana, Chreste, quod facis lingua.

[You carry hairless testicles, Chrestus, and a cock like a vulture's neck and a head smoother than prostituted arses; there is not a hair alive on your shins and the cruel tweezers purge your white jowls. But your talk is of Curios, Camillus, Quinctius, Numa, Ancus, and every hairy worthy we ever found in books; you are loud and threatening with big words, and you quarrel with the theatres and the times. If, as this goes on, some young athlete comes your way, now freed from tutelage, whose swollen penis has been unpinned by the smith, you summon him with a nod and lead him off; and I shouldn't like to say, Chrestus, what you do with your Catonian tongue.]

Whatever a *"Catoniana lingua"* might be, it seems clear that Chrestus's sexual activities are to be deemed "unacceptable" (see no. 10 again). What we are shown first, however, is a bald grotesque with bizarre genitals (see no. 3). But Chrestus's real vice is hypocrisy (no. 6): Curio, Camillus, and the rest are (or, rather, were by Martial's time) real people, important figures in the Roman tradition. To these, and the other "hairy worthies," Chrestus gives lip service in public, but when the right young fellow comes along, he gives another sort of "lip service" entirely—conduct hardly worthy of a *vir bonus*, much less of a man who loudly proclaims the virtues of Roman manhood. (A *vir bonus*, by the way, is a "good" man not in the sense of his being in the state of grace, but of being "a good man for the job." *Vir*, of course, is the root of "virile" and of "virtue," in the sense of the Italian *virtù*, and so might better be translated as something like *hombre* or *Mensch*.)

The epigram at book 9.57 is aimed at one Hedylus:

> *Nil est tritius Hedyli lacernis:*
> *non ansae veterum Corinthiorum,*
> *nec crus compende lubricum decenni,*
> *nec ruptae recutita colla mulae,*
> *nec quae Flaminiam secant salebrae,*
> *nec qui litoribus nitent lapilli,*
> *nec Tusca ligo vinae politus,*
> *nec pallens toga mortui tribulis,*
> *nec pigri rota quassa mulionis,*
> *nec rasum cavea latus visontis,*
> *nec dens iam senior ferocis apri.*
> *res una est autem—ipse non negabit—*
> *culus tritior Hedyli lacernis.*

[Nothing is worn smoother than Hedylus's cloak: not the handles of old Corinthian bronzes, not a shin polished by a ten-year shackle, not the skinned neck of a ruptured mule, not the ruts that cleave the Flaminian Way, not the pebbles shining on the beaches, not a hoe polished by a Tuscan vineyard, not the yellowing gown of a dead pauper, not the shaken wheel of a lazy muleteer, not a bison's flank shaven by the cage, not the aging tusk of a ferocious boar. One thing, however—and he won't himself deny it—Hedylus's arse is worn smoother than his cloak.]

The pertinent loci here seem to be nos. 3 and 4 ("physical appearance," "eccentricity of dress"), with no. 10 implied by the smoothness of Hedylus's arse. But it is the way this epigram is put together and the path by which Martial gets to the punchline that is of more interest to us here. "Nothing [*nihil*] is worn smoother . . . *except* one thing [*res una . . . tamen*]—his arse," arrived at via ten lines of "nots," is a brilliant use of the old strategy of "not, not . . . *but*." Readers have to work through a long list of some pretty bizarre examples of smoothness (the *ruptae recutita colla mulae* or the *rasum cavea latus visontis*, for example), with expectation intensified as they anticipate the "but." Notice also the way in which the whole is framed by *"nil est tritius"* at the beginning and *"tritior"* at the end (something Martial also does in 7.20: *"nihil est ... gulosius"* in the first line, *"gulosus ille"* in the last).

One last example, an then we can begin drawing some conclusions about how Martial's insults "work." Book 1.92:

> *Saepe mihi quaeritur non siccis Cestos ocellis*
> *tangi se digito, Mamuriane, tuo.*
> *non opus est digito: totum tibi Ceston habeto,*
> *si deest nil aliud, Mamuriane, tibi.*
> *sed si nec focus est nudi nec sponda grabati*
> *nec curtus Chiones Antiopesve calix,*
> *carea si pendet lumbis et scripta lacerna*
> *dimidiasque nates Gallica paeda tegit,*
> *pasceris et nigrae solo nidore culinae*
> *et bibis immundam cum cane pronus aquam:*
> *non culum, neque enim est culus, qui non cacat olim,*
> *sed fodiam digito qui sperest oculum:*
> *nec me zelotypum nec dixeris esse malignum.*
> *denique pedica, Mamuriane, satur.*

[Cestus often complains to me with tears in his eyes of being touched by your finger, Mamurianus. No need for the finger; have Cestus complete, Mamurianus, if he is all you lack. But if you have neither fireplace nor bare bedframe, nor a broken cup of Chione or Antiope, if the cloak that hangs from your loins is yellowed and patched and a Gallic jacket covers half of your buttocks; if your only food is the smell of a blackened kitchen and you drink dirty water on your belly with the dog: why, I shall dig my finger into—not your arse, for an arse that never shits is none at all—but your remaining eye. And don't call me jealous or malevolent. In short, Mamurianus, sodomize on a full stomach.]

It is not easy to see what is going on here. The poet seems to be encouraging Mamurianus to persist in his pursuit of Cestus, "if he is all you lack" (*si deest nil aliud*); and having sex with young boys (which is what Cestus appears to be doing, *"non siccis ocellis"*) was not a shameful activity in Martial's Rome. So it is difficult to read this as an insult (in spite of the temptation to see loci nos. 4 and 10 hinted at), although it might be construed as a criticism. What catches the eye, however, is the argument Martial has put together, one influencing the tradition represented by Marvell's "To His Coy Mistress" in its "If . . . then" structure: "If he is all you lack [then go ahead]" and "If you are living in pathetic and sordid conditions, then I shall poke you in the eye. [But you are not.] So carry on," *denique pedica . . . satur*—something close, I should say, to the old *modus tollens* form of proof ("If *p*, then *q*. But not *p*, therefore not *q*"). What is important about such an argument structure, however, is not the degree to which it can be rigorous or convincing, but the way in which it plays on the listener's expectations. In this sense, Martial does here the same sort of thing that we saw him do in, e.g., 9.57 and 7.20; and if argument structures are in question, a second look at the Sosibianus and Mammeia couplets will turn up two abbreviated "syllogistic" arguments—enthymemes. One begins to understand why one of his most avid Renaissance readers, Julius Caesar Scaliger, considered the epigram the most "deductive" of poetic forms.

The appeal to loci ("what everybody knows") and the manipulation of expectation and fulfillment (the "conclusion") are, in short, at the heart of the designs behind Martial's epigrams, particularly those whose aim is to insult.

But what of the targets of Martial's insults? Do they deserve such treatment? It should be noted that none of the characters in the particular epigrams we have looked at was a real person. There is no question that there were in Rome people who engaged in the bizarre behaviors Martial describes; but Hedylus, Chrestus, Santra, Mammeia, and the rest are fictions. So Martial has deployed the technical devices at his disposal—from the inventory of stock topics to the small-scale stylistic devices we just glanced at—to compose pungent and devastating insults directed at people who didn't exist! I do not think this was because he was afraid of insulting real people known to his readers. What we are seeing in these short pieces are technical displays on the order of the declamations that were so important in rhetorical training in his day.

This would suggest that one of the main reasons his *libelli* proved

so popular was the virtuosity they exhibited. An audience of sophisticated readers who knew, for instance, the epigrammatic tradition in
which he worked showed their appreciation for Martial's literary skills
by continuing to purchase his poems and, no doubt, to look forward
to the next available booklet. But there is perhaps more to it than that.
One recent explanation for his popularity in Rome (as well as in future
eras) points to the priapic motif in Martial: Priapus, the ithyphallic god
of sexual potency, serves as a symbol of dominance and control, and
Martial's criticism of women who are given to "unnatural acts," of effeminate homosexuals, old people, and gluttons all arises from his desire to dominate others. This, then, is why his style is so aggressive and
severe—and perhaps snide. This desire, presumably, would be shared
by many, if not all, of Martial's sophisticated readers, and such a presumption would indeed make sense in the sort of social and political
milieu in which they operated—"patriarchal," some would say, in the
extreme. (See "Martial the Moral Jester: Priapic Motifs and the Restoration of Order in the Epigrams," by Eugene O'Connor, in *Toto Notus in
Orbe*, ed. Farouk Grewing (Stuttgart, 1998), 187–204.)

It is hard to imagine an appeal more basic than a shared desire for
dominance, particularly sexual dominance. But I think this approach
overlooks an important element of agreement in its attempt to explain
Martial's apparent aggressiveness. While reading Martial, we are, as it
were, looking over his shoulder as he points to the disreputable and
disgusting Santras and Mammeias around him. We, too, disapprove of
their activites, and we, too, are put off by their appearances, their stu-
pidities, and their hypocrisies. We are on Martial's side—or, rather, he
is on ours. And he is very good at what he does, much better than any
"normal" person could be. What is more, we *want* to be on his side—or
rather, to have this master of invective on our side. Now this may be
because we, as readers, want also to be sexually dominant, as Martial
appears to be. But that is only part of it. Martial speaks of "what everybody knows"; and "everybody knows" that stupidity and hypocrisy are
not limited to, or even best symbolized by, sexual activity. Think of the
political threats represented by Cicero's Catiline or Antony—or, rather,
of how Cicero gets us on his side against them. So Martial's "nauseous"
epigrams do pit "us against them"; but they manage to do just that, it
appears, by their indirect assertions of communal values, not simply
by asserting "mine's bigger than yours."

The Domestication of Sir John Falstaff

Shakespeare's plays teem with expert insulters of all occupations and social standing, from Prince Hal to Kent, whom we saw earlier, to Doll Tearsheet of the Boar's Head Tavern in Eastcheap. We also saw earlier that it is necessary always to keep apparent insults in their situational perspective. So, for instance, Doll Tearsheet in *Henry IV, Part II*,

> I scorn you, scurvy companion. What! You poor, base, rascally, cheating, lack-linen mate! Away, you moldy rogue, away! I am meat for your master. (2.4.131ff.)

—these lines to the unfortunate Pistol, who has been so bold as to suggest a toast to her health. She continues,

> Away, you cutpurse rascal! You filthy bung, away! By this wine, I'll thrust my knife in your moldy chaps an you play the saucy cuttle with me. Away, you bottle-ale rascal! You basket-hilt stale juggler, you! (136ff.)

This is all, of course, in character, just the sort of vituperation one might expect of an East London barmaid—although it does not appear, by the way, that Shakespeare consulted the Insult Kit in writing her lines: not a single term of abuse appears in the online kit's lists. Earlier in the same scene, Prince Hal seems also to be an accomplished insulter. Speaking to Francis, the potboy, he says,

> Wilt thou rob this leathern-jerkin, crystal-button, not-pated, agate-ring, puke-stocking, caddis-garter, smooth-tongue, Spanish-pouch (77ff.)

But we must be careful. The epithets here are also absent from the lists of the kit, but rightly so. "Not-pated," for instance, simply means "with hair cut short"; and "puke" here means "gray." Hal is referring to the accoutrements of an innkeeper, not insulting one. On the other hand, Hal shows his talents clearly in an exchange with Falstaff early in *Henry IV, Part I*:

> There is a devil haunts thee in the likeness of an old fat man, a tun of man is thy companion. Why dost thou converse with that trunk of humors, that bolting hutch of beastliness, that swollen parcel of

dropsies, that huge bombard of sack, that stuffed cloak-bag of guts, that roasted Manningtree ox with pudding in his belly, that reverend vice, that gray inquiry, that father ruffian, that vanity in years? Wherein is he good, but to taste sack and drink it? Wherein neat and cleanly, but to carve a capon and eat it? Wherein cunning, but in craft? Wherein crafty, but in villainy? Wherein villainous, but in all things? Wherein worthy, but in nothing? (2.4.481ff.)

This is not only intense, as insults go, it is rhetorically polished: notice the similes regarding Falstaff's obesity, and the *gradatio* at "cunning . . . craft . . . crafty . . . villainy . . . villainous." But here, too, we must be careful. Hal is here taking a part in a little "play" he and Falstaff are putting on for the Boar's Head crowd, and his insults are not meant seriously.

Earlier in this same scene, however, we see Hal and Falstaff going at it over Falstaff's outlandish version of the outcome of a failed scheme:

HAL: I'll be no longer guilty of this sin—this sanguine coward, this
     bed-presser, this horseback-breaker, this huge hill of flesh—
FALSTAFF: 'Sblood, you starveling, you elf skin, you dried neat's
     tongue, you bull's pizzle, you stockfish. Oh, for breath to utter what
     is like thee! You tailor's yard, you sheath, you bow case, you vile
     standing tuck— (267ff.)

An exchange like this seems highly irregular. After all, Hal is *Prince* Hal, royalty, and Falstaff a commoner; and Falstaff knows that Hal is a prince. This has already been taken care of by Shakespeare, however. From the beginning of the play we know that Hal is acting like "one of the boys" and willing to engage in barroom banter as such; and we know why. As Hal explains in his soliloquy at the end of act 1, scene 2,

> I know you all, and will awhile uphold
> The unyoked humor of your idleness.
> Yet herein will I imitate the sun,
> Who doth permit the base contagious clouds
> To smother up his beauty from the world . . .
> . . . By so much shall I falsify men's hopes,
> And like bright metal on a sullen ground,
> My reformation, glittering o'er my fault,
> Shall show more goodly and attract more eyes

Than that which hath no foil to set it off.
I'll so offend, to make offense a skill,
Redeeming time when men think least I will.

(1.2.218–40)

We do not know Hal's plan when he and Falstaff first enter at the beginning of act 1, scene 2. In fact, we don't even know who they are or what we should expect of them then—or, perhaps more importantly, Shakespeare's audience didn't know. Falstaff addresses Hal by name, it is true: "Now Hal," he says, "what time of day is it, lad?" And "Hal" replies with,

> Thou art so fat-witted, with drinking of old sack and unbuttoning thee after supper and sleeping upon benches after noon, that thou hast forgotten to demand that truly which thou wouldst truly know. What a devil hast thou to do with the time of day? Unless hours were cups of sack, and minutes capons, and clocks the tongues of bawds, and dials the signs of leaping-houses and the blessed sun himself a fair hot wench in flame-coloured taffeta, I see no reason why thou shouldst be so superfluous to demand the time of day. (1–13)

From these, the first words we hear from Hal, we learn a great deal. First, the fat man we behold (and there is no reason to believe that the original Falstaff was not indeed fat) is a drunk, a glutton, and a lecher. Immediately after (14ff.), we learn that this fat man is also a thief by night—or claims to be; and a little after that (110–11), we learn that Hal might join Falstaff in some nocturnal caper. We also learn from the opening lines of the scene that Hal is capable of eloquent vituperation. Not only does his insult begin with a Ciceronian triplet ("drinking," "unbuttoning," and "sleeping") and continue with a series of ingenious similes (a little later, an ability explicitly admired by Falstaff), it is an enthymeme. So Hal is a character with considerable intellectual and rhetorical skills—and royalty, to boot, as Falstaff makes clear a few lines later.

The connections between our perceptions of stylistic practice and dramatic character are—or should be—fairly obvious. For instance, early in act 1 of *Henry IV, Part II*, the chief justice has this to say about Falstaff's pretense of youth (at 1.2.171ff.):

Do you set down your name in the scroll of youth, that are written down with all the characters of your age? Have you not a moist eye? A dry hand? A yellow cheek? A white beard? A decreasing leg? An increasing belly? Is not your voice broken? Your wind short? Your chin double? Your wit single? And every part about you blasted with antiquity? And you yet call yourself young? Fie, fie, fie, Sir John! (1.11.221–29)

—another enthymeme, one backed up by an artistically composed topical enumeration of parts (and notice the play on contraries, e.g., "moist"/"dry," "decreasing"/"increasing," etc.), capped by "single," i.e., "feeble." Of course, the chief justice is a judge, and judges are supposed to be able to make eloquent arguments based on evidence. So the lines Shakespeare gives to him are certainly in character—character that the audience can understand only by hearing how, as well as what, the character speaks. We shall have more to say about such matters shortly.

But let us return to Falstaff. As in *Part I*, Falstaff makes his first appearance in *Henry IV, Part II* in scene 2 of the first act, accompanied by his (evidently very small) page. Shakespeare's audience would have recognized him immediately. But this is not the Falstaff promised at the end of *Part I*, where Falstaff's last lines are "I'll purge, and leave sack, and live cleanly as a nobleman should do" (5.4.168–69). In his first fifty lines he insults three different individuals: the page himself ("Thou whoreson mandrake, thou art fitter to be worn in my cap than to wait at my heels" [16–17]); his tailor, Mr. Dombledon ("Let him be damned, like the glutton! Pray God his tongue be hotter! A whoreson Achitophel! A rascally yea-forsooth knave!" [39–41]); and Prince Hal, from whom we learn a little later he has been "severed" (1.2.227–28):

the juvenal, the Prince your master, whose chin is still not fledged. I will sooner have a beard grow in the palm of my hand than he shall get one on his cheek, and yet he will not stick to say his face is a face royal. God may finish it when He will, 'tis not a hair amiss yet. He may keep it still at a face royal, for a barber shall never earn sixpence out of it, and yet he'll be crowing as if he had writ man ever since his father was a bachelor. (22–30)

The Hal of *Part II* is, of course, not the same Hal as the Hal of *Part I* either. It is he who has "left the sack and lived cleanly as a nobleman should do." But Falstaff is much the same as he was: ready to abuse in the company of an inferior, but courteous—almost courtly—in the presence of a superior, such as the chief justice, who enters shortly after Falstaff's tirade against his page and the others (see lines 104ff.). And what we see as the play goes on is the emerging authority and decisiveness of Prince Hal as he prepares to take his ailing father's place on the throne. As some critics have put it, Hal becomes more "kingly" and less "princely"; and in the process, he distances himself more and more from Falstaff and his sidekicks until, at the end (5.5.51ff.), he can look Falstaff in the eye and say,

> I know thee not, old man. Fall to thy prayers.
> How ill white hairs become a fool and jester!
> I have long dreamed of such a kind of man,
> So surfeit-swelled, so old, and so profane,
> But being awaked, I do despise my dream.
> Make less thy body hence, and more thy grace.
> Leave gourmandizing. Know the grave doth gape
> For thee thrice wider than for other men.
> Reply not to me with a fool-born jest.

And in the sequel, *Henry V*, Bardolph, Nym, Pistol, and Mistress Quickly all come back; but Falstaff does not, as he is reported to be ill at the end of act 2, scene 1, and to have died at the beginning of 2.3. Shakespeare, in short, kills him off.

Of course, that is not really the end of Falstaff, for he has a leading part in *The Merry Wives of Windsor*, produced some time after the *Henry IV* plays and possibly after *Henry V*. Whatever the chronology, it is clear that Shakespeare, whether on his own or because of popular demand, saw fit to bring Falstaff to the stage again—not quite the same Falstaff, but Falstaff nonetheless.

Before we turn to *Merry Wives of Windsor*, though, we need to back up a bit and remind ourselves of a few things. Up until now, we have concentrated our attention on the insults traded among Shakespeare's characters and looked briefly at their formal characteristics. Now we need to pay more attention to the theatrical setting, to how Shakespeare uses insults—among many other devices, obviously—to shape our attitudes toward his characters and the things they do, and thus to inform our expectations, both of the play's line of action and of the parts played by the characters in moving that action forward.

In traditional plays, at least, the playwright needs to make matters clear at the outset in order to enable the audience to follow the action and to care enough about the characters in the play to stay around to see how it all comes out. Audiences need to have early answers to the paramount questions, "What?" and "So what?" Accordingly, a playwright makes two kinds of "contracts" with the audience. The first we might call a "fire engine" contract—when you hear the siren, and the siren gets louder, you expect to see the fire engine come around the corner. And you expect, after its arrival, that the firefighters will perform certain acts, eventually putting out the (putative) fire. This is what generic conventions help to do: let us know, in general, what to expect; and it is what prologues like the one at the beginning of *Romeo and Juliet* or at the beginning of act 2 of *Henry V* do. Breaching this contract is forbidden, although violations of dramatic expectations can often be an effective way of surprising one's audience or of inviting critical reflection on the conventions themselves—what Brechtian alienation seeks to do, for instance. But toying with one's audience's basic expectations can result in theatrical disaster, for the most part.

The other kind of contract we might call an "ethical" contract, one part of which centers on how we will expect a certain character to operate and the other part of which relates to the "So what?" question: why should we be "for" or "against" a given character? Why should we care about what a character does in the course of the play? Some of this ethical contract is built into the fire-engine contract or generic conventions; but more frequently, and more importantly, our attitude toward a character is shaped by what that character says and does, and how he or she says or does it. Our attitude may also be shaped by what other characters say about or do to the character in question. The playwright, in short, needs to create a network of allegiances between the audience and the characters. Here the notion of violating or breaching the contract may be less of a problem than the violation of dramatic expectations (the structural equivalent of *paraprosdokian*, i.e., surprise). Many plays, after all, are about character development. But what is important to bear in mind is that, when a character undergoes some change for the better or for the worse, it is in terms of our *initial* assessment of the character that we approve or disapprove. But what is even more important to remember is that it is the playwright—Shakespeare, in the present instance—who makes up the characters, who have, of course, no lives of their own.

Having said all this, let us look at the opening (1.1) of *The Merry Wives of Windsor*.

Windsor, before the Page family house. Enter Justice Swallow, Slender, and Sir Hugh Evans.

SHAL.: Sir Hugh, persuade me not. I will make a Star Chamber matter of it. If he were twenty Sir John Falstaffs, he shall not abuse Robert Shallow, Esquire.

SLEN.: In the County of Gloucester, Justice of Peace and "Coram."

SHAL: Aye, Cousin Slender, and "Custalorum."

SLEN.: Aye, and "Ratolorum" too; and a gentleman born, Master Parson, who writes himself "Armigero," in any bill, warrant, or obligation. "Armigero."

SHAL.: Aye, that I do, and have done any time these three hundred years.

SLEN.: All his successors gone before him hath done't, and all his ancestors that come after him may. They may give the dozen white luces in their coat.

SHAL.: It is an old coat.

EVANS: The dozen white louses do become an old coat as well. It agrees well, passant. It is a familiar beast to man, and signifies love.

SHAL.: The luce is the fresh sigh. The salt fish is an old coat.

SLEN.: I may quarter, Coz.

SHAL.: You may, by marrying.

EVANS: It is marring indeed, if he quarter it.

SHAL.: Not a whit.

EVANS: Yes, py'r lady. If he has a quarter of your coat, there is but three skirts for yourself, in my simple conjectures. But that is all one. If Sir John Falstaff have committed disparagements unto you, I am of the Church, and will be glad to do my benevolence to make atonements and compremises between you.

I have supplied the G. B. Harrison's stage directions and attributions (though not the glosses on obscure words); but we must remember that such editorial helps were not available to Shakespeare's audience. All they saw were three men, one, presumably, in clerical garb, enter and take the stage. Now for the "contracts." We learn names, to begin with: Sir Hugh (a parson); Robert Shallow, Esquire; Cousin Slender. We also learn that Robert Shallow, Esquire, is intent on bringing some legal action against Sir John Falstaff, whose reputation was presumably known by the viewers of the play. A little later, Anne Page and her father, Master Thomas Page, are mentioned (45), and Evans (whose surname we have not yet learned) says (55ff.), "It were a goot motion if we leave our pribbles and prabbles and desire a marriage between Master Abraham and Mistress Anne Page." Who is Master Abraham? We do not learn this until line 240 (it is Slender); but so far we can expect some sort of confrontation with Falstaff and a marriage plan. Such are the stock elements of a domestic comedy. So we have been supplied, in just 35 lines or so, with information and some general expectations. Unless Shakespeare is fooling us with dramatic misdirection, we know, roughly, where we are headed.

The ethical contract—or, rather, contracts—is more a matter of showing than of telling. Shallow obviously thinks highly of himself, as his inclusion of "Esquire" and his reference to the family coat of arms ("Armigero" is the designation of a gentleman with a coat of arms) and three hundred years of tradition. Slender is a confused and not very bright man, as his misunderstanding of "luce" (which, by the way, means "pike," as in the fish) and the mixing up of "successors" and "ancestors" show; and Evans is not much brighter, as he hears "louse," "a familiar beast to man," instead of "luce." We soon learn more about Evans, as we hear more lines delivered by him: "py'r lady," and, later, "fear of Got," "device in my prain," "that fery person for all the orld," and "pribbles and prabbles"—that is, he is a Welshman with a less than certain grasp of the English tongue. In short, we have before us a legal eagle, a dunce, and a foreigner, with all the expectations that go along with such stock figures. Shakespeare has thus put on stage some hotshots and lowlifes—stock comic roles—with a plan—a stock comic plotline.

Shakespeare does pretty much the same thing a couple of scenes later, in 1.4. There (4–6) we are introduced to the servant of Doctor Caius (Mistress Quickly, but we don't learn that immediately) and to Peter Simple, Slender's servant (18). Of Doctor Caius, Mistress Quickly announces (5–6), "here will be an old abusing of God's patience and the King's English"; and when he enters at line 45, we see (or hear) what she is talking about:

> Vat is you sing? I do not like des toys. Pray you go vetch me in my closet *un boitier vert*—a box, a green box. Do intend vat I speak? A green-a box.

Simple has come to try to persuade Mistress Quickly to convey a proposal of marriage to Anne Page from Slender (!), and is hiding from Caius in a closet, where he is discovered:

> O *diable, diable!* Vat is in my closet? Villain! Larron!
> ... Peace-a your tongue—Speak-a your tale. (70–71, 84–85)

Caius thinks, mistakenly, that Evans intends to propose to Anne Page, and sends Simple off with his own letter:

> By gar, it is a shallenge. I will cut his troat in de park, and I will teach a scurvy jackanapes priest to meddle or make. You may be gone. It is not good you tarry here—By gar, I will cut all his two stones. By gar, he shall not have a stone to throw at his dog. (1.4.116–19)

"By gar," he says after Simple exits, "I will myself have Anne Page," thus complicating the marriage plotline even more.

By the end of act 1, in short, Shakespeare has set the action of the play in motion and introduced us to the players, among whom are two foreigners, a loudmouthed lawyer, and a fool aptly named Simple, who is servant to the equally foolish Slender.

These are objects of comic derision, to be sure; but it is interesting to notice the overlap between the grounds for our thinking these characters worthy of derision (comic or otherwise) and the loci of invective we saw in connection with Cicero and Martial. Foreign or otherwise inferior origins, pretentiousness, stupidity, and, in the cases of Evans and Caius, something very close to oratorical ineptitude—not to mention physical appearance and eccentricity of dress—are stock topics of abuse in a rhetorical tradition with which Shakespeare was quite familiar; and it is not farfetched to imagine that he had such commonplaces in the back—perhaps in the forefront—of his mind when he conceived these characters and set them before his audience.

But what of Falstaff? As we saw, he is mentioned in the very first lines of the play. He enters at line 112, kisses Mistress Ford at line 200, and then leaves, not to be seen again until scene 3. There we see him in a familiar setting, a room in the Garter Inn, in the company of Bardolph, Nym, and Pistol. And there we are presented with another fire-engine contract when Falstaff says, "I must cony-catch. I must shift" (36–37), and outlines a scheme to "make love to Ford's wife": "she gives the leer of invitation," but, more importantly, she "has all the rule of her husband's purse," as does also Mistress Page: "She bears the purse, too. She is a region in Guiana, all gold and bounty. I will be cheaters to them both, and they shall be exchequers to me" (75–78). And so, "varlet vile" that he is (so Pistol, 106), he dispatches Pistol and Nym with letters Falstaff has addressed to both of the women.

The contents of the letters are revealed in the exchange between Mistress Ford and Mistress Page at the beginning of act 2, where it comes out that both women have received the same billet doux, and thus Falstaff's plan begins to unravel. Pistol and Nym betray the scheme to their husbands, who plot their response in turn—deceiving the deceiver. Ford, disguising himself as one Master Brook (2.2.150ff.), persuades Falstaff (with the promise of even more money) to assist him in his own attempt to seduce Mistress Ford, and what follows are the memorable scenes in which Falstaff is hidden in a laundry basket, takes on a couple of preposterous disguises, is exposed and, at the end, forgiven.

This is not, in short, the same Falstaff Shakespeare's audience might have expected. Instead of a commanding character, he is merely a compliant instrument in the service of a conventional melodramatic plot in a play where the audience knows more than any of the characters. It is worth noticing that insults are almost entirely absent in the play after the end of act 1. True, there are scenes in which Shakespeare is having fun with his characters—the Latin lesson at 4.4, for instance, and the laundry basket scene—but making a character ridiculous is not quite the same as subjecting that character to ridicule. The only signs of the old Falstaff appear in a brief exchange with Pistol at the beginning of 2.2, and in a passage that reminds us of the Falstaff of the *Henry* plays toward the end:

Hang him [Ford], poor cuckoldy knave! I know him not. They say the jealous, wittolly knave hath masses of money, for the which his wife seems to me well-favored. I will use her as the key of the cuckoldy rogue's coffer, and there's my harvest home . . .

Hang him, mechanical salt-butter rogue! I will stare him out of his wits. I will awe him with my cudgel. It shall hang like a meteor over the cuckold's horns. Master Brook, thou shalt know I will predominate over the peasant, and thou shalt lie with his wife. (2.2.281–86, 290–96)

Of course, he knows not who it is he is insulting. But we do—it is Ford himself, in the guise of Master Brook, to whom these lines are addressed. And so it is also for the rest of the play, through the complications to the dénouement, until the final scene of the play, where Falstaff finally begins to learn what we have known all along: as she points to the horns Falstaff is wearing as part of his final disguise, Mistress Page says,

Now, good Sir John, how like you Windsor wives?
See you these, Husband? Do not these fair yokes
Become the forest better than the town?
FORD: Now, sir, who's a cuckold now? Master Brook, Falstaff's a knave,
    a cuckoldy knave. Here are his horns, Master Brook. And Master
    Brook, he hath enjoyed nothing of Ford's but his buck basket, his
    cudgel, and twenty pounds of money, which must be paid to Master
    Brook. His horses are arrested for it, Master Brook.
MISTRESS FORD: Sir John, we have had ill luck. We could never meet.
    I will never take you for my love again, but I will always count you
    my deer.
FALSTAFF: I do begin to perceive that I am made an ass.
FORD: Aye, and an ox, too. Both the proofs are extant. (5.5.110–27)

And so, having seen the error of his ways, the contrite Falstaff is pardoned; and, as in the old Roman comedies, proper social relations are restored (including the successful courtship by Master Fenton of "sweet Anne Page"), and all is well:

MISTRESS PAGE: Well, I will muse no further. Master Fenton,
    Heaven give you many, many merry days!
    Good Husband, let us every one go home
    And laugh this sport o'er by a country fire,
    Sir John and all.

FORD: Let it be so, Sir John,
   To Master Brook you yet shall hold your word,
   For tonight he shall lie with Mistress Ford.

Thus the domestication of Sir John Falstaff.

There is nothing very original in these observations. But our intention was never to present a novel or unconventional interpretation of *The Merry Wives of Windsor* and its relation to the *Henry* plays. It is what those plays can teach us about insult that is our concern. Accordingly, it might be useful to end here with a brief summary of the lessons we have learned. First, we can see the importance of situation. But there are two situations that need to be attended to: the situation within the play (who is insulting whom, and why) and the situation in the theatre, wherein Shakespeare presents us with various characters drawn according to the classic commonplaces of invective. The converse, of course, is also true. Shakespeare draws other characters along the lines of the commonplaces of praise. In playing upon these loci, Shakespeare is able to shape our attitudes toward and collective expectations of the characters and what they do. And the loci of invective are there: lowly occupation, gluttony and the rest, oratorical ineptitude, and physical appearance, which is not simply a matter of staging but is worked into the dialogue. We find also a rich storehouse of terms of abuse (none of them, as far as I can see, in the Insult Kit) and unmistakable signs of rhetorical sophistication in the style and argumentative structure of many of the insults in these plays. But what may be most striking about the insults in these plays is the role of social status: those of superior status have no problem insulting their inferiors; but if inferiors insult their superiors, they do it behind their backs. Falstaff himself is, of course, the prime example.

"I shall taunt you a second time-a!": Monty Python

One of Britain's greatest gifts to Western civilization is *Monty Python's Flying Circus*. *Monty Python* grew from half-hour collections of absurd comic skits into various absurd comic feature-length movies, such as *The Life of Brian* and *Monty Python and the Holy Grail*. Although they are not nearly as topical or biting as more recent (and animated) programs such as *The Simpsons* and *South Park*, the humor that came from the team of writers behind (and performing in) *Monty Python* is in many ways more zany and penetrating than anything that has come along since the 1960s. And an important component of that humor is insults—some of them, it might be added, distinctly Shakespearean.

In one early episode—a "black-out routine," really—a man in a good suit knocks on an office door (I will occasionally have to supply some stage directions). An angry man opens the door:

ANGRY MAN: WHADDA YOU WANT?

MAN: Well, I was told outside that . . .

AM: DON'T GIVE ME THAT, YOU SNOTTY-FACED EVIL PAN OF
DROPPINGS!

M: What?

AM: SHUT YOUR FESTERING GOB, YOU TIT! YOUR TYPE MAKES ME
PUKE! YOU VACUOUS STUFFY-NOSED MALODOROUS PERVERT!

M: YES, but I came here for an argument!!

AM: OH! Oh! I'm sorry! This is abuse!

M: Oh! I see!

AM: Aha! No, you want room 12A, next door.

M: Oh! Sorry!

AM: Not at all . . . [*under his breath*] stupid git!

Explaining a joke, we all know, is the surest way of ruining it. If the person you explain it to didn't get it the first time, he or she won't get it even if you explain why it is *supposed* to be funny. So let us begin by concentrating, again, on the insult aspects of the exchange. The Man's "gob" is not, of course, festering at all, nor is he "snotty-faced." "Gob," "tit," and "vacuous" are all in the family of terms of abuse—even if you don't truly understand what "gob" means, or "tit" in this situation (but it sounds like "twit"). On the other hand, a "snotty-faced evil pan of droppings" (not "drippings"!) or a "malodorous pervert"—ingenious choices of epithets, it occurs to one—might well make one want to "puke." Our initial bewilderment as to why the Angry Man should attack Man—it is, as they say in the theatre, "unmotivated"—clears up when we learn that the confrontation is taking place outside of something like the Department of Abuse ("Abuse 'R' Us"?), with a Department of Argument next door. That is, "abuse" and "argument" are commodities or services handled by professionals of sorts: "Oh.! I'm sorry! . . . You want 12A, next door." The professional in the skit, it will be noted, draws on the loci of personal appearances (including body odor) and sexual practices; but at the same time, once Man's mistake becomes clear, the two are quite civil to one another—until the very end, where it appears that Angry Man is not so professional, after all. As weird as the situation played out is, however, it will be familiar to anyone who has had to deal with "professionals" in some office or other. So it makes sense.

Another early skit takes place in a butcher shop. Actually, it needn't take place in a real butcher shop (or a stage set of one):

GENT: Good morning! I'd care to purchase a chicken, please.

BUTCHER: Don't come here with all that posh talk, you nasty, stuck-up twit.

GENT: I beg your pardon?

BUTCHER: A chicken, sir. Certainly.

GENT: Thank you. And how much does that work out to per pound, my good fellow.

BUTCHER: Per pound, you slimy trollope, what kind of ponce are you?

GENT: I'm sorry?

BUTCHER: 4/6 a pound, sir, nice and ready for roasting.

GENT: I see, and I'd care to purchase some stuffing in addition, please.

BUTCHER: Use your own, you great poovy po-nagger!

GENT: What?

BUTCHER: Ah, certainly, sir, some stuffing.

GENT: Oh, thank you.

BUTCHER: "Oh, thank you," says the great queen like a lah-di-dah poofta.

GENT: I beg your pardon?

BUTCHER: That's all right, sir, call again.

GENT: Excuse me.

BUTCHER: What now, you great pillock?

GENT: Well, I can't help noticing that you insult me and then you're polite to me alternately.

BUTCHER: I'm terribly sorry to hear that, sir.

GENT: That's all right. It doesn't really matter.

BUTCHER: Tough titty if it did, you nasty spotted prancer.

Here we have what might be called a critique of "shop etiquette," which requires civility between those doing business, above all, civility

of the shopkeeper toward the customer. Ordinarily, calling a customer a
"poovy po-nagger" or a "la-di-dah poofta" would constitute a breach of
decorum. It is our shared sense of what is appropriate in a shop setting
that this exchange seems to question. (In this connection, one recalls
that there is a popular restaurant in Chicago at which the waiters and
waitresses routinely insult the customers, who are said to find it very
entertaining.) However, the Butcher may be right to make fun of the
Gent, whose "I'd care to purchase" and "per pound" are indeed "posh
talk" and whose demeanor is perhaps overly polite even though Gent
obviously thinks of himself as Butcher's superior. For his part, Butcher,
when he is being "polite," encourages this, with his repeated "sir" and
seeming apology just before the end. Even if we do not know what a
"po-nagger" is, moreover, we do know what "stuck-up twit," "ponce,"
and "poofta" mean (they are quite British terms), and we do know what
it means to call a man a "trollope" and a "queen." So in addition to the
class relations implicit in the shopkeeper/customer exchange, we see
the Butcher insulting his customer as effete and homosexual; and if we
share Butcher's attitude toward effete homosexuals, we are on his side.

What all this is getting at is the complex of shared understandings and values that underlie this skit—this *comic* skit, I should add. A
more complicated complex of understandings, values, and what educators call "preknowledge" is called for in the case of this scene from
Monty Python and the Holy Grail:

SCENE 8 [*King Arthur music, sound of horses*]

ARTHUR: HALT! [*sound of horns*] Hallo! [*pause*] Hallo!

GUARD: Allo! 'Oo is eet?

ARTHUR: It is King Arthur, and these are my Knights of the Round Table. Whose castle is this?

GUARD: Thees ees the castle of my master, Guy de Loimbard.

ARTHUR: Go and tell your master that we have been charged by God
with a sacred quest. If he will give us food and shelter for the night,
he can join us in our quest for the Holy Grail.

GUARD: Well, I'll ask him, but I don't think he'll be very keen. Uh, he's
already got one, you see.

ARTHUR: What?

GALAHAD: He says they've already got one!

ARTHUR: Are you sure he's got one?

GUARD: Oh, yes. It's very nice-a. [*To other guards:*] I told him we already got one. [*Guards chuckle.*]

ARTHUR: Well, umm, can we come up and have a look?

GUARD: Of course not! You are English types-a!

ARTHUR: Well, what are you, then?

GUARD: I am French! Why do you think I have this outrageous accent, you silly king-a?

GALAHAD: What are you doing in England?

GUARD: Mind your own business!

ARTHUR: If you will not show us the Grail, we shall take your castle by force!

GUARD: You don't frighten us, English pig-dogs! Go and boil your bottom, sons of a silly person! I blow my nose at you, so-called Arthur King, you and all your silly English k-nnnnniggets. Thpppt! Thppt! Thppt!

GALAHAD: What a strange person!

ARTHUR: Now look here, my good man—

GUARD: I don't wanna talk to you no more, you empty-headed animal food trough wiper! I fart in your general direction! Your mother was a hamster and your father smelt of elderberries!

GALAHAD: Is there someone else up there we could talk to?

GUARD: No. Now go away, or I shall taunt you a second time-a! [*Sniffs.*]

ARTHUR: Now, this is your last chance. I've been more than reasonable.

GUARD: Fetchez la vache!

OTHER GUARD: Quoi?

[*Mooing.*]

ARTHUR: If you do not agree to my commands, then I shall—

[*Loud mooing. The rear end of "la vache" appears at the top of the castle wall, and a large clump of manure comes down.*]

JESUS CHRIST!

KNIGHTS: Christ! [*Thud.*] AH! OOH!

ARTHUR: Right! CHARGE!

KNIGHTS: CHARGE!

[*Mayhem ensues.*]

GUARD: Hey, this one is for your mother! There you go! . . . And this one's for your dad!

Attending first to the explicit insults in the scene, we note that the Guard ridicules the ancestors of the English as "silly persons," "hamsters" and "smelling of elderberries," and the English themselves as "pig-dogs" and "empty-headed animal food trough wipers"—classic (Classical) topics of invective. More, the guards' insults go beyond the verbal: "I blow my nose at you," "I fart in your general direction"—gestures that, though neither classic nor Classical, are easily grasped. And then, of course, there is the manure dropped from the top of the castle wall.

As for the situation: Monty Python's audience was undoubtedly familiar with the general outlines of the Arthur and Knights of the Round Table stories, with Arthur himself, Sir Galahad, Guinevere, Lancelot, Merlin, and the rest—including the Holy Grail—from exposure to the many versions in childrens' books, serious novels, musicals (*Camelot*, which, it will be remembered, inspired the journalistic characterization of the Kennedy White House as "Camelot"), and the like. And perhaps some of the members of the audience knew, or knew of, Thomas Malory's fifteenth-century *Morte d'Artur*. To appreciate the scene, in other words, the audience had to have a pretty detailed knowledge or recollection of the Arthur story. And if they knew Malory, they would know that he was a rough contemporary of the historical Henry V, and that Henry was victorious at the famous battle fought with the French at Agincourt. If they knew those things, they may also know that the original version of the Arthur story goes back at least to the twelfth century, in the romances of Chrestien de Troyes. At that level, the scene might be read as a critical confrontation of the English cultural claims implicit in their version of the Arthur story with the cultural claims of the French in theirs. Or, if the audience were familiar with *The Merry Wives of Windsor*, they would recognize that the Guard's accent ("nice-a," "types-a," "king-a," "second time-a") is just like that of Doctor Caius in that play. And, as in the Shakespearean theatre, Monty Python's audience would be inclined to support Arthur and disdain his French opponents—or at least understand that support of Arthur is one of the premises of the movie. Finally, some members of the audience—members of an older generation—might also have picked up on the similarity between the name of the castle's owner and a bandleader famous half a century ago, Guy Lombardo.

In short, the audience of this scene and the other skits we looked at must have a deep familiarity with the institutions, lore, and values that lie behind them in order to get the jokes they are telling. A similarly deep familiarity with institutions, lore, and values is necessary in knowing an insult when we see one.

Let us explore this juxtaposition of jokes and insults a little. Earlier we explored Ted Cohen's observation that a joke is a successful transaction only when the teller and the listener implicitly acknowledge a shared background. This implicit acknowledgment is the foundation, he says, of a kind of intimacy that develops when one's joke succeeds. This is what we mean when we say that when a joke falls flat, the teller may assume that the listener doesn't share the teller's "sense of humor."

In order to get a better idea of what Cohen is talking about, let us look at a joke told to me once by a colleague:

> The Father, the Son, and the Holy Spirit planned, finally, to take a vacation, and were sitting around trying to decide where to go. "Mesopotamia," the Father volunteered. "It's a beautiful place, there between the Tigris and Euphrates. I haven't been there since I kicked Adam and Eve out of the Garden." "No, no," said the Son. "I think we should go to Bethlehem. I was too young to appreciate it when I left, and I'd like to see what it is like. After all, it is my place of birth."
>
> They both looked to the Holy Spirit.
>
> "What do you say?" they asked in unison.
>
> "Rome," the Holy Spirit replied. "I've never been there."

Clearly, in order to begin to get this joke, you need to be familiar with the doctrine of the Trinity in its conventional Father–Son–Holy Spirit form (which is in only one passage in scripture, Matthew 28:19) and with the stories told in Genesis and Matthew or Luke (none of which is mentioned in the telling). It also helps to know where the Tigris and Euphrates are. There may be some readers who don't know these things, and so don't laugh. Notice, too, the set up at the beginning. You know this will be a three-step joke with the Holy Spirit getting the punchline. This joke has what Kenneth Burke calls rhetorical form: the arousal of expectations and their fulfillment. The form and the content are inseparable, too, which you can see once you start playing around with the order or attribution of lines: it would not make sense to have the Son being nostalgic for Mesopotamia. The joke's premise, taken out of context, is, however, far from being theologically correct, as it posits not only the three persons of the godhead being in need of a vacation but disagreeing with one another. The three persons of the Trinity seem more like Homeric (or perhaps Lucianic) gods than the God referred to in the Nicene Creed. But let us consider all that just an instance of lighthearted anthropomorphism.

The punchline is another matter, however. This is not a joke that could be characterized as pro–Roman Catholic or pro-pope, as the Catholic Church has long held itself and its pope to be inspired by the Holy Spirit, the ultimate source of the church's authority and the pope's infallibility. It is, pretty clearly, a Protestant joke.

Whether it is a good joke is a complicated matter. Do you have to agree with what the Holy Spirit says to think it funny? If you are a devout Roman Catholic, you might think it not very funny and in rather bad taste if a Protestant, knowing that you are Catholic, told you this joke. On the other hand, if one Catholic told it to another Catholic, both might laugh, but more because of the incongruities in it—especially the incongruous Holy Spirit saying he'd never been to Rome. If a Catholic told it to a Protestant, the Protestant would laugh both because of the incongruities and because he never thought the Holy Spirit had ever been in Rome. If a Protestant told it to another Protestant, the joke would not only be funny, it would be an implicit way of rejecting the authority of the Catholic Church and, more, of the pope himself. That's what the Reformation was all about. And that, if you keep in mind the strife the Reformation brought to sixteenth- and seventeenth-century Europe, makes it a darker sort of humor altogether. In short, whether or not it is a good joke—indeed, just what the joke is—is a deeply situational matter embracing the teller, the audience, their shared beliefs and values, and the propriety of the joke.

The matter of propriety points up one of the intersections between jokes and insults and reminds us of some of the observations we made about situation at the beginning of this book. If the joke were told by a Protestant to a devout Catholic, we would be seeing a misplaced presumption—a violation, perhaps, of the sort of intimacy Cohen writes about—and so also a sort of social gaffe, a faux pas. The joke would probably not work because the Catholic didn't share the Protestant's "sense of humor," and the Catholic's failure to appreciate the joke, much less laugh at it, might be perfectly valid. The Catholic might, indeed, find the joke insulting. (On the other hand, one can imagine a principle of "identification" that would enable the Catholic to transcend partisan theology and appreciate the joke for what it was intended to do [get a laugh] and for the skill that went into its composition. It is just this sort of variable identification that makes it possible to admire Donne's "Death Be Not Proud," a poem giving little consolation to one who does not believe in an afterlife but which still can be recognized for the masterpiece it is. We will have more to say about such matters later.)

In telling jokes, then, as in trading insults, one must be very careful about one's audience. There is no doubt that Monty Python's skits and movies were meant primarily for a British audience. Shopkeepers and office workers are a common experience in every developed country, and so the spectacle of one of them insulting a customer is familiar in its incongruity, and the humor is accordingly quite portable. *Monty Python and the Holy Grail* is a different matter, however. A French audience might not find the scene we looked at very funny at all, any more than a Welshman or a Frenchman might have found Evans and Caius in *The Merry Wives of Windsor* very funny. It is one thing to say to a British audience that Evans "abuses the King's English"—a remark that cues the attitude Shakespeare wants us to have toward him—and quite another to show to a Welsh audience one of their own doing so. I know no French person who has felt insulted by Monty Python's *Holy Grail*, but I can easily imagine one. And it is a matter of record, and not speculation, that a good number of devout Christians were insulted by another Monty Python movie, *The Life of Brian*, a spoof on the story of Jesus. (For the Pythons' side of the story, see the site at http://www.videosift.com/ video/The-Secret-Life-Of-Brian-Monty-Pythonreligion-documentary; or, more recently, Michael Palin's account in his *Diaries, 1969–1979: The Python Years* (New York, 2006), in the entries for 1979. Palin says *The Life of Brian* was banned that year in South Carolina, for instance.)

Just Add a Dash of Theology

A friend of mine once told me that if you want to make a nasty disagreement even nastier, just add a dash of theology. The Protestant Reformation and the Catholic reactions to it resulted in bitter dispute of unprecedented geographical range and chronological endurance, and the level of vitriol was, if not unprecedented, then not surpassed, either. The Reformation, then, seems like a good place to look for examples of insults; and, in fact, it is such a good place that we can hardly do it justice here.

One has only to glance at the thousands of *Flugschriften*—"flyers," i.e., pamphlets—that were in circulation all over Europe, beginning in the early sixteenth century and lasting well into the seventeenth (or later!) to get a taste of the sort of thing the polemicists on both sides were able to cook up. The title of Luther's *An den christlischen Adel deutscher Nation von den christlischen Standes Besserung* (*To the Christian Gentry of Germany and the Improvement of Its Standing as a Christian Nation*, Wittemberg, 1520) is pretty tame, but it doesn't take long for Luther to call the pope *"die rot hür von Babilonien"* ("the red whore of Babylon," which would be used after Luther by all his fellow antipapists—until the present day, it might be added, if we recall the words of Dr. Paisley of Belfast) and to dismiss the papal curia as *"ein hurhaus ubir alle hurhewsser"* (*sic*: "the whorehouse to beat all whorehouses"). The insults in this literature, on all sides of the conflicts that the Reformation stirred up, are, in short, pretty harsh and colorful.

So it is that we find Heinrich von Kettenbach asserting in 1523 that Catholics are nothing but *"die Römischen stalbuben und linsenscheisser"* ("Roman stablehands and window-washers") and *"dreck und laymen des Bapst"* ("trash, flunkies of the Pope"), not to mention *"weibische Zodomitische buben"* ("effeminate, sodomite rogues"), and their beliefs *"ein jauf"* ("a big joke"). And a little later, in 1526, the Catholic polemicist Johann Cochlaeus describes Luther's teaching as *"teufliche,"* *"Ketzerische,"* *"lugenhaftig,"* *"unverschempt,"* and *"lausig"* ("satanic," "heretical," "deceitful," "shameless," and "lousy"). Animal metaphors abound. To Kettenbach, Catholics are *"kotzende Hunde"* ("puking dogs") and the pope himself, a *"reissender Wolf"* ("ravenous wolf"). The pope is often (as in the pamphlet coauthored by Luther and Melanchthon, *Deutung der czwo growlichen figuren*, 1523) depicted as an ass, or as having an ass's head. To the Catholic Hieronymus Emser, Luther is *"das wild geyffernd Eberschwein"* ("that uncultivated savage wild boar"), but to Thomas Müntzer, he is a *"tückischer Fuchs"* ("a sly fox").

One of the more interesting devices employed by these authors are puns on names. "Eck," for instance, becomes *"Geck"* ("conceited ass"); "Murner" becomes *"Murnarr"* ("grumbling buffoon"); "Cochlaeus" becomes "*Kochleffel*" ("ladle"); "*Aristoteles*," "*Narrestotile*" (a *Narr* is a jester or a buffoon); and "Luther" becomes "*Luder*" ("whore") in a 1522 Leipzig *Flugschrift* by Wolfgang Wulfer, *Wid' die unselige auffrure Merten Luders*, and frequently thereafter. "Emser" became "*Bock*" (billy goat) by way of the printer's device on the cover of his 1521 response to Luther's *An den Christlischen Adel*: a goat with the legend "*Hut dich der Bock stosst dich*" ("Beware! The goat butts"). Luther's "*Antwort*" to Emser, "*Auf des bocks zu Leypczick*," begins, "*Lieber Bock stosst mich nicht*" ("beloved Bock does not butt me"), and Emser is referred to as "Bock" from then on. (See, on these figures, M. M. Guchmann, *Die sprache der deutschen politischen literatur in der zeit der Reformation und des Bauernkrieges* (Berlin, 1974), which is more about the regional dialect differences in the *Flugschriften* than about the events that gave rise to them.)

A similar range in the terms of abuse can be seen in the French equivalents to the *Flugschriften* that appear in the second half of the sixteenth century during the religious wars and persecution of the Huguenots, works with titles like *Complainte et chanson de la grande paillarde babylonienne de Rome* (Jean Chassagnon, s.l., 1561)—which shows that the "whore of Babylon" canard was still alive and well in France; or, from the other side, *Les Combatz du fidelle papiste, pelerin romain, contre l'apostat priapiste vivant à la synagogue de Genève, maison babilonicque des luthériens* by the famous Catholic polemicist Artus Désiré (Rouen, 1550); or *La singerie des Huguenots, marmots et guenons de la nouvelle secte theodobeszienne, contenant leur arrest et sentence par jugement de raison naturelle* (Paris, 1574—i.e., after the St. Bartholomew's Day Massacre) by the Franciscan Thomas Beauxamis: "The monkey tricks of the Huguenots, the little long-tailed apes of the Theodobezian sect (a reference to Theodore Beza), including their arrest and sentencing by order of natural reason." The Franciscans seem to have been favored targets of Protestant insults, represented either as heretics, as in Conrad Badius's *L'Alcoran des Cordeliers* (i.e., Franciscans), *tant en latin qu'en François. C'est-à-dire, la mer des blasphèmes et mensonges de cest idole stigmatisé qu'on appelle saint François* (Geneva, 1560); or (at great length) as sexual predators, as in Henri Estienne's 1566 *Apologie pour Hérodote*, chapters 22–24 (in vol. 2 of P. Ristelhuber's 1879 Paris edition, 6–72). (There is an excellent survey of the pertinent literature in Claude Postel's *Traité des invectives au temps de la réforme* [Paris, 2004].)

Further investigation turns up Lambert Daneau's sensational *De deux monstres prodigieux à savoir d'un Asne-Pape qui fut trouvé à Rome en la rivière du Tibre l'an MCCCXCVI et d'un Veau-Moyne nay à Friberg en Misne l'an MDXXVIII* (Geneva?, 1557) (*Of Two Prodigious Monsters: An Ass-Pope Found in Rome in the River Tiber in 1396 and a Monk-Calf Born in Freiburg in 1528*); and the ex-Capuchin Bernardino Ochino's *L'image de l'Antichrist* (1544), in which the supporters of the pope are described as a society composed of "*loups, ours, lions, chiens muetz, aspicz sourds, dragons, leopards, bestes, generation de serpens*" ("wolves, bears, lions, mute dogs, silent vipers, dragons, leopards, beasts, a generation of serpents")—a veritable bestiary of epithets.

As we have seen, animal terms are a standard part of the insulter's arsenal—and so they are here, in French religious polemic. We find, in addition to the ones we've just seen in the titles of Daneau and Orchino, terms like *babouin, chaméleon, conil* ("rabbit"; also *lapin*), *porc, scorpion, singe* (as in Beauxamis's "*singérie*"), and *vermine*—among others. Some are rarely encountered (*babouin*, for instance, usually in the phrase "*baiser le babouin*," "to kiss the baboon," i.e., submit in humiliation), others quite frequently: *aspic* ["viper"], *chien* ["dog"], *loup, singe*, and *vipère*. Some have both positive and negative connotations: *lion*, for instance, can connote ferocious courage or simple ferocity. *Chaméleon* can refer to prudence and adaptability or to lack of principle. Even *chien* has both positive (dependability) and negative (as in "dirty dog") applications, as has *asne*, which is sometimes a symbol of sturdiness. Most have associations that go back to scripture (the *vipère*, for instance), others to the medieval *Physiologus* tradition of allegorical bestiaries. *Vipére, singe, porc, vermine*, and *loup* are evidently always negative and, interestingly, almost always used by Protestant writers to describe Catholics, particularly priests.

Terms of abuse are not, of course, limited to such animal metaphors. We find a great number, for instance, that assert moral inferiority, if not outright criminality: *coquin* ("good-for-nothing"), *excrément, ruffien, bandolier* ("bandit"), *brigand*, and the like. And, of course, there are many related to "sinful" behavior: *ivrogne* ("drunk"), *fripeline* ("guzzler" or "glutton"), *cafard* ("hypocrite," but sometimes "cockroach"), *ribaude* ("slut"), *golaffre* ("debauché"), and *putain* ("whore"), for instance; or to more depraved sexual activity: *priapiste* and, as frequently, *bougre* (as in buggery). Both of these last terms, like *singe* and *ivrogne*, are directed almost exclusively toward Catholic clergy by Protestant writers. And this list is far from complete.

At this point, we might pause and remind ourselves of just what we are looking at in this body of literature from Reformation Germany and France. It represents, first of all, an enormous volume—the first instance, many have observed, of mass communication. The numbers are not easy to come by, but the inventories of titles and printers of the German material in *Flugschriften aus der Reformationszeit* fill twenty volumes (printed between 1877 and 1953, and still being supplemented), including an entire volume taken up by the exchanges between Luther and Hieronymus Emser and another by Luther's pamphlets attacking *Die Schwärmer*, the Anabaptists, whom he compared to a swarm of gnats. Mind you, the lists are of titles, each of which was printed and distributed in hundreds, if not thousands, of copies. The print run of Luther's *An den christlischen Adel*, for instance, seems to have been in the neighborhood of four thousand. So the total number of copies of *Flugschriften* from both sides was enormous. As for the French equivalents, there is no standard catalogue of everything published in the sixteenth century, but Postel's index (in *Traité des invectives*, cited earlier) lists the names of over two hundred authors and printers of religious controversialist works, and his survey and analysis cover more than three hundred titles, which he admits is far from exhaustive.

These pamphlets, accordingly, reached a huge number of readers— and, by the way, were nothing if not economically viable for their printers—all across Europe. There were far fewer "readers," of course, than "nonreaders," illiterates into whose hands these pamphlets, by design, found their way. For both the literate and the illiterate, illustrations were provided, mainly in the form of woodcut engravings, some by the most prominent artists of the time, such as Albrecht Dürer. These engravings, then, not only complement the texts to which they were added; in many cases they were substitutes for the text. And what is interesting about them in the present instance is the degree to which they paraphrased visually, if you will, the texts they accompanied.

This is not always the case, to be sure. But it is clear that Dürer and the rest often availed themselves of a visual vocabulary that was synonymous with the lexicons of abuse we have seen in the German and French material. While we can't possibly produce here (or anywhere,

Der Bapſteſel zu Rom

for that matter) a comprehensive survey of visual synonyms, a few examples will serve to make the point and suggest that words and pictures were seen as two cooperative vehicles for confessional conflicts and the insults they engendered.

The first example is this engraving depicting the "Ass-Pope" in the pamphlet by Melanchthon and Luther mentioned earlier, *Deutung der czwo growlichen figuren*. This was reprinted often enough to become a virtual commonplace (no doubt it is behind, for example, Daneau's *De deux monstres prodigieux à savoir d'un Asne-Pape qui fut trouvé à Rome en la rivière du Tibre*). The head is that of an ass, symbol of obstinacy and ignorance. The scaly body brings to mind a serpent, symbol of evil familiar to us from Genesis, of course. The bared breasts bring to mind the whore of Babylon, so common in Reformation iconography, based on Apocalypse 17:1. The right arm is in the shape of an elephant's foot, symbol of the crushing oppression of souls exercised by the papacy. Coming out of the left hip is the face of an old man looking backwards toward the past. The tail, in the shape of a dragon's head, spits fire, as the papacy spits out edicts and papal bulls. The right foot is cloven, as is Satan's; and the left, with its talons, symbolizes the rapacity of the Catholic clergy. All of this would, of course, be explained to those who did not understand the picture and who could not read Melanchthon's explanations.

This engraving is found in a pamphlet detailing the evils of Catholicism that appeared about 1568 and has been attributed to Tobias

Abzeichnus etlicher wolbedencklicher Bilder võ Römischen abgotsdienst

Im Mönster zu Straßburg/ gegen dem Predigstl Iober/nében dem Chor/ober dem Gang/ da etliche Adeliche Schildehangen/ in Stein in ein Capitalsenl geharven: Vnd in betrachtung/ das deß Mönsters Fundament im Jahr Christi 1015. geleat vnd folgenden 1277. Jahrs biß an den Thurn vollendet worden: Vor mehr dann dreyhundert Jahren dahin für ein Seul Pasament gesetzt.

Stimmer (1539–84). In it, we see depicted most of the animal imagery that comprises the bestiaries so often alluded to in the literature of the time, both Protestant and Catholic. The upper left panel shows a "procession" performed by a bear (symbol of cruelty: see, e.g., Deuteronomy 7:2–5), a wolf (savagery, deception; see, e.g., Genesis 49:27), and a rabbit (cowardice, but also sexual activity). The wolf is almost ubiquitous in the anti-Catholic literature: bishops are routinely *loups rabis* (rabid wolves) in French materials, for instance. The upper right panel shows a dog (voracity, servility—and compare the many French references to *les chiens Sorboniques*) or a fox (slyness, deceit) on a litter borne by a boar (the *"Eberschwein"* of the *Flugschriften*, symbol of savagery and depravity alike) and a goat (depravity, sexual appetites, etc.; Matthew 25:32, for instance), with a monkey in attendance (the *marmot* of the French pamphlets? In any event, symbol of sex, rapacity, gluttony; 2 Chronicles 9:21, for instance). The lower left shows a deer (luxury, but sometimes, in the Latin play on *cervus*, represented as a pun on *servus*, or "serf"), presumably at the moment of consecration during the Catholic Mass. And the lower right panel has a monkey holding a book (scripture?) read by an ass, images that by now should be self-explanatory. In short, we have here a compendium of insults by way of animal imagery, all of which are amplified upon in the text printed below the illustration.

The Thirty Years' War pretty much brought an end to such business on the Continent, but not so in England, where religious strife continued well into the seventeenth century. Much of that had little to do with Reform, as such, but had much to do with English politics, a prominent motif of which continued to be antipapalism. This comes out clearly in an engraving in John Vicar's "Behold Romes [*sic*] monster on his monstrous Beast," which appeared in 1643, six years before the beheading of England's Catholic monarch Charles I. (The engraving is reproduced in J. P. Malcolm's 1813 *An Historical Sketch of the Art of Caricature, with Graphic Illustrations*. The original is now in the British Library. Vicars (1580–1652), author of eulogies of Oliver Cromwell, was a radical Presbyterian Calvinist.)

The iconography is different from what we saw earlier, but much of it is rather conventional: the tiara (A), for instance, the Seven Deadly Sins represented by a seven-headed (rather generic) beast (D), and the skeletons symbolizing Death (N). The excretions coming out of "The

Barrell of Sinne" (H) are fairly common in earlier Continental illustrations, but they are identified in the explanatory "poem" attached to the picture as "the dregs and lees / Of Rome's all-rotten reliques, dear decrees"; and the vessels held by those below (I) are specified as "cups of Romish fornication." Similarly, the figures at G and K, we read, are "The Babel's bishops, Jesuits, friers base"; and "Serjeant Death" (N) is said to drag "Rome's monster on his monstrous beast" toward "the pit / Of desolation and destruction dire." The storm cloud in the upper right corner represents "Heaven's indignation," which "Pours down the phials of dire desolation / Upon Rome's w—— [*sic*]"—i.e., The Whore of Babylon is still around. Thus, the symbols that are not self-explanatory are glossed for the viewer by the doggerel that accompanies them.

These engravings are obviously meant to do more than just spread the Word. By providing vivid images and drawing on the lexicon of abuse, they depict the opposition (in our examples, Catholics; but the same is true of the opposite side) as "the Other"—grotesque beasts, biblical symbols of evil, *das Scheusal*, *der Feind*. Kenneth Burke once "quoted" an imaginary critic as saying, "I know you are a Christian, but who are you a Christian against?" These pictures let their viewers know "who they are against," but in doing so, they also create a view held *in common* by the viewers. Being against Catholics and the pope is what defines their identity. And so what we are seeing here (to borrow another phrase from Kenneth Burke) is an instance of "yea-saying by nay-saying"— something we saw earlier in the case of Cicero, for instance. This, of course, was also the function of the *Flugschriften*, meant as they were not only to defame the opposition but to strengthen the bonds of the faithful, whether to the pope or to the Reformation.

Lines and Storylines

Our brief look at some of the engravings accompanying religious polemic in the Reformation era suggests that we might briefly sketch out what some of the lessons we learned from our examples of verbal insult might reveal when applied to visual materials such as caricatures and cartoons, comic strips, or even animated cartoons. I say "briefly sketch" because a moment's thought is enough to remind us that, first of all, the amount of potentially pertinent visual material is staggering. We cannot hope to cover here more than a few examples. A moment's thought also reminds us that even a "straightforward" political cartoon, for instance, is open to elaborate and lengthy rhetorical exegesis. It is not only difficult to know where to start—it is even more difficult to know where to stop.

But let us start with a couple of "straightforward" political cartoons. Consider first this one:

This represents President George W. Bush as being nothing more than a ventriloquist's dummy for Karl Rove. The inspiration for it probably originated with the allegations that, during a 2004 presidential debate, Bush had an audio wire under his suit jacket to relay questions and responses to him while the debate was going on. Consistent with the conceit, Rove, who is clearly labeled, is much bigger than the Bush dummy and has his hand, literally, under Bush's jacket. What makes the cartoon work, of course, is the widespread belief among those opposed to Bush that he was, in fact, not very smart (a "dummy") and dependent upon Rove, who was seen as something of an evil genius. The cartoon, then, has the effect of illustrating that to be the case. It is an

Cartoon by J. D. Rowe of *The Mobile Register*, found at http://cagle.slate.msn.com.

insult that aims at pleasing the anti-Bush people and dismaying his supporters.

If all that seems too obvious to dissect, consider the next example:

Here we have Bush pouring the tea and asking Cheney ("Dick") what to do, and Cheney giving orders. Again, Bush is the smaller figure, Dick's inferior. The cartoon makes reference to debates over changes to Bush's cabinet at the start of Bush's second term, and the implication is that Cheney is the one who is truly in charge—another belief common among Bush's opponents. But notice that the conceit here is drawn from *Alice in Wonderland*, with Bush playing the bungling White Rabbit and Cheney the Mad Hatter. With the mushrooms visible at the right, behind Dick, we may also be reminded of the scene with the imperious hookah-smoking Caterpillar ("It means whatever I say it means"). Mike Lane was clearly depending on the readers' familiarity with the masterpiece by Lewis Carroll—and perhaps even with the Disney version of it. Without such a familiarity, a reader would undoubtedly be puzzled by this cartoon, even if aware that Cheney is there depicted as being in charge of Bush's administration, to the president's detriment.

At this point, we might recall Cicero's characterization of Catiline's associates or his vivid description of Antony vomiting on the dais and his continued assertions of Antony's stupidity—the point of which

Cartoon by Mike Lane of the *Baltimore Sun*, found at http://cagle.slate.msn.com.

was, after all, to rally the senate and the Roman people to his side and against Antony's. Instead of calling on the commonplaces of political invective that Cicero employed, Rowe and Lane allude to images familiar from popular entertainment known to all of their readers. Or consider the amount of "prior knowledge" the writers of the Arthur scene in *Monty Python and the Holy Grail* assumed on the part of their audience. Or the depiction of the opposition as less than human that we saw in the *Flugschriften*—we even have a rabbit, and a rather preposterous one at that. In short, we see the intimacy that insult assumes in order to execute a put-down of the opposition and consolidate the identity of the partisans of the insulter.

A deeper level of intimacy is required for this wordless cartoon by the Swedish artist Gustave Ewert Karlsson:

To begin with, obviously, one must be aware of who is being caricatured (students I showed this one to had no idea) and recognize that Margaret Thatcher is dressed up as Winston Churchill ("Winnie"), with his trademark cigar, top hat, and cane. John Major wears a woman's suit, an oversized hat, and shoes too big. Major, students of recent British history might recall, was a surprise nominee for Thatcher's successor as prime minister, supported by Thatcher but not well-known even to the British press. Depicting the two as cross-dressers, as Karlsson does, amounts to a harsh assessment of the two politicians, especially of Major. Certainly, it was Thatcher's desire to project a Churchillian image, as the Falkland Islands adventure made abundantly clear. But the argument of the cartoon seems to turn on what Aristotle called a "proportional metaphor": Thatcher (of whom François Mitterrand once said, "She has the mouth of Marilyn Monroe and the eyes of Caligula") is to Churchill as Major (said by the historian Paul Johnson to be "a man from nowhere, going nowhere, heading for a well-merited obscurity") is to Thatcher. And, to be sure, it was Major's promise to carry on Thatcher's "legacy" (as far as anyone knew, he had himself no distinctive policies) that the Tory Party, but not necessarily the rest of Europe, found reassuring.

Another cartoon, by the famous Gillray, the subject of T. Wright's meticulous 1870 *Works of James Gillray, the Caricaturist, with the Story of*

In J. Szabo and J. A. Lent, *Cartoonometer: Taking the Pulse of the World's Cartoonists* (North Wales, PA, 1994), 100; reproduced here by permission from WittyWorld Books, Inc.

The Corsican Crocodile dissolving the Council of Frogs!!! 10th Brumaire i.e. 9 November

His Life and Times, calls for even more knowledge of the historical situation it intends to represent.

Here the artist seems to be drawing on the bestiary tradition, with Napoleon, "The Corsican Crocodile," dissolving the French Council of Five Hundred in November of 1799 ("18th Brumaire, i.e., 9 November" in lower left-hand corner), an event well publicized in the British (and, of course, in the French) press at the time. Knowing the story is crucial. On his return from his campaigns in Egypt (hence the crocodile), Napoleon found Paris in an uproar, with rumors of an impending coup d'état and collapse of the government. Napoleon persuaded the senators of the Council of Ancients, who had been gathered together in the Tuileries, to name him, by decree, commander in chief of the troops in and around Paris, and then he announced a state of emergency. On November 10, he stormed into a meeting of the council (whose members are represented here as frogs) being chaired by his brother, Lucien, with a detachment of grenadiers (the other crocodiles, to the left). After a scuffle in which Napoleon was himself physically assaulted,

Napoleon ordered his grenadiers to fix bayonets and clear the room. As they marched into the chamber, it is reported, many of the terrified deputies jumped through the windows and crowded through the doors. (See the account in Louis Madelin, *The Consulate and the Empire* [London, 1939], 1–23.) Napoleon, of course, was not yet emperor. That would not happen for five more years. But Gillray understood the significance of Napoleon's actions on 18th Brumaire (the one referred to by Marx in his account of the second 18th Brumaire as "a tragedy"), and placed a crown on Napoleon's head, since by dismissing the council he became de facto ruler.

Cartoons in newspapers have proven to be an effective means of rallying support during times of war, often by the simple device of depicting the enemy as subhuman or even monstrous—much as they did during the Reformation. Consider, for instance, a cartoon by Grant Hamilton from 1898, just after the explosion that sunk the *U.S.S. Maine* in Manila Harbor, the incident that sparked the Spanish-American War.

The Spanish Brute Adds Mutilation to Murder

If the imagery is not self-explanatory, the artist (like those in the *Flugschriften* we saw earlier) helps by adding labels.

War cartoons from more recent decades regularly depict the enemy as an Other: Germans, during World War I, as Huns; Japan, during World War II, as an octopus; the USSR, during the cold war, as a forbidding bear. Interestingly, Saddam Hussein, during the two conflicts that had the U.S. making war in Iraq, was seldom depicted as subhuman—crazed and ugly, perhaps, but not an ugly animal. Of course, such depictions are not limited to war cartoons. Venezuela's Hugo Chavez, for instance, has not fared very well at the hands of cartoonists recently, and the U.S. has not been at war with Venezuela. And Vladimir Putin makes an occasional appearance as a weasel.

The rhetorical function of such depictions is, in any case, pretty obvious.

If cartoons provide us with examples of a visual mode of insult, comic strips provide much more. They have story lines and characters, and much of what we were able to say about insults in Shakespeare and *Monty Python* can be said as well about some comic strips. I have in mind one such strip that ran for over forty years in newspapers across the U.S. and had a readership that at its height is estimated to have been in the neighborhood of 50 million: Al Capp's *L'il Abner*. (A selection can be found in Al Capp, *The Best of L'il Abner* [New York, 1978]. The images reproduced here have received permission from Capp Enterprises, Inc.)

L'il Abner was born in the darkest days of the Great Depression, in 1934, and provided its readers with a combination of slapstick comedy and social criticism by tracing the fortunes of L'il Abner, Mammy and Pappy Yokum (his parents), Daisy Mae Scragg (the love interest who would become Abner's wife), Moonbeam McSwine (like Daisy Mae, a statuesque, curvaceous young woman), Earthquake McGoon ("the world's dirtiest wrestler"), and several others who live in "Dogpatch." They are stereotypical hillbillies who, were it not for occasional attractive qualities, might easily be the subjects of several of the loci of invective we saw earlier: embarrassing family background, physical appearance, eccentricity of dress, oratorical ineptitude, and gluttony and drunkenness, for instance. But in the hands of their creator, they be-

come a vehicle for some serious satire of middle-class America, including the politicians produced by it.

It is not possible to reproduce a whole L'il Abner strip here, but perhaps a summary of one will suffice to illustrate some of the aspects of
insult we have already seen and add some aspects we have not. "Snapples" (*Best of L'il Abner*, 120–27) begins with a frame showing Abner
reading about "Slobbovia," a place where the inhabitants' "favorite
dish is polar bears and vice-versa," a place so miserable that "It'll make
yo' app-ree-she-ate Dogpatch," as Abner puts it. As it happens, all that
the soil of Slobbovia is good for is growing "snapples," a fruit that "re-
werses [*sic*] the ageing process: One Snapple and—snap!—you're 17
again!" The scene shifts to the office of Senator Jack S. Phogbound,
who has just discovered that he trails in a poll taken in Dogpatch, dead
last, behind Helen Gurley Brown and Henny Youngman. To improve
his standing, he decides to "revive the U.S. economy" by collecting "th'
8 billion Rasbuckniks Slobbovia owes us," which "not even the smart
Dogpatchers" will know are worthless. Phogbound flies to Slobbovia, where he is greeted by natives who speak a Russo-Yiddish sort of
English.

Phogbound witnesses the rejuvenating effects of eating snapples
(Capp came up with this word long before the popular drink by the

same name hit the market) and offers to cancel Slobbovia's debt in return for its snapple crop. At seventeen, he explains, "no one expects you to work or be in your right mind: the American dream come true!" Back in Washington, various officials sample the snapples and turn seventeen again, to their delight. On witnessing this, the president (LBJ, as it happens) orders them impounded in Fort Knox lest the nation become "one big Berkeley campus." Bitterness and frustration spread among the "forgotten citizens"—working adults—who demand loudly for "Middle Age Power": "Wouldn't it be wonderful when mommies and daddies are hippies, too?" asks a mother. The son replies, "It'll be a drag! Who'd feed us, bail us out and clean up the flowers we toss around?" And the last frame shows the president biting into a snapple himself, saying, "If you can't fight 'em, join 'em."

Capp's critique is, obviously, aimed at middle-class America, even more at the youth, and perhaps most of all at politicians, all of them foolish enough to prefer to make of America "one big Berkeley campus." Of course, to understand Capp's critique, one would have to know what "Berkeley campus" connotes (noisy disorder, if not drug-induced depravity), and one would have to know also who Helen Gurley Brown and Henny Youngman (editor of *Cosmopolitan* and kitsch comedian, respectively) were. But more interesting is the way Capp manipulates hierarchies: middle-class America puts down the hillbillies of Dogpatch, who in turn put down Slobbovians. That is before snapples enter the picture. Post-snapples, it appears that the grotesquely ugly and desperately poor Slobbovians, who speak poor English (and are meant to bring to mind Russians?), are honest, wise (they want nothing to do with snapples, as no seventeen-year-old could possibly get fat enough to survive Slobbovia's arctic climate), and, in their strange way, law abiding, holding a trial, as they do at one point, to decide whether one of their number should be subjected to "snappital punishment." They are in fact morally superior to Americans, older, younger, and, particularly, in political office—more or less in that order. Whether they are superior to the denizens of Dogpatch is unclear (although there appears no Slobbovian "Earthquake McGoon"). But what Capp has done is inverted the hierarchy that has Slobbovians being put down, and he has put down instead the "superior" class, the president (LBJ) above (below?) all.

Doing the Dozens

In "doing the dozens," a form of verbal dueling popular in African American culture, two competitors (usually, but not always, young men) try to outdo one another in insults. An example (constructed from exchanges recorded by Onwuchenkwa Jemie in his *Yo' Mama!* [Philadelphia, 2003], 160–88) follows:

A: Yo, man. Your hair hurtin'? It sure looks nappy.

B: Yeah? Well I saw yo' mama yesterday, and she sure was lookin' raggedy.

A: Yeah, well yo' mama wears dirty drawers.

B: Hell, yo' mama don't wear panties AT ALL.

A: Yo' mama so ugly she hurts my feelings.

B: Yo' mama looks like her face caught fire, and someone tried to put it out with a brick.

A: Yo' mama looks like she was beat with a ugly stick.

B: Yo' mama sent her picture to the lonely hearts club and they sent it back and said "We ain't THAT lonely!"

A: Man, yo' mama's ass is so big she has to wear suspenders to hold up her drawers.

B: Yo' mama's ass is so big that when she walks down the street it looks like two bears rasslin' under a blanket.

A: Man, when you were born they put you on the stoop to see whether you'd bark or cry.

B: Hell, man. If I had dog with a face like yours, I'd shave its ass and make him walk backwards.

A: You smell so bad, the last time you took a bath the soap fainted.

B: You so low down you need an umbrella to keep off the ant piss.

A: Your family's so poor, yo' mama goes to church, puts in a penny, and asks for change.

B: Yo' papa's so poor he can't even pay attention.

A: Your house is so small that when I go in the front door I fall over the back fence.

B: I went to your house and stepped on a roach and yo' mama said "There goes dinner!"

A: You ain't got no roaches. The rats ate them all.

B: Your family's so poor the roaches leave at dinnertime.

A: Yo' mama wears Puerto Rican roach killers: shoes so pointy she can stomp roaches in the corner.

B: Man, you so dumb, if brains was food you'd starve to death.

And so it goes on—and on. The insults traditionally focus on personal appearances, sexuality, standing in the community, and, of course, "Yo' mama"—a theme that, while not mandatory, is perhaps the most characteristic one encountered. One notes also how large a part hyperbole plays in the insults. The game ends either when the audience of onlookers declares one of the players the winner or when one player can no longer respond to the other's insults—or when the game degenerates into a fistfight, or worse.

The origins and social function of this game are obscure. Some have traced the practice back to West Africa, others to the slavery period in African American history, and the game has been variously explained as a way of letting off the steam generated by "black rage" or as a nonviolent way of asserting superior status, via skill in ex tempore insults—or as both. It is clear, however, that being good at the dozens is a sign of a sort of social superiority.

The dozens has attracted considerable attention recently. A program called *Yo' Mama* was produced for and broadcast by MTV. In it, two contestants are invited by the master of ceremonies to trade insults back and forth, with a small group watching, cheering, and encouraging the contestants. When the dozens session ends, the audience votes on who is the winner. The insults are, naturally, carefully monitored, so as to keep the FCC from charging the program with having obscene content. More than simply being monitored, the insults are far from extemporaneous, as the contestants have ample notice and are able to prepare—those parts, that is, that are not already scripted. The participants (cast?) are racially diverse, and the setting (set?) is a beach somewhere in Southern California. The result, one is quick to decide, is quite bland and contrived.

In another area of black popular culture, that of "battle rap" or "beefing," we hear echoes of the dozens. In the 2002 motion picture *8 Mile*, for instance, we witness two rappers, Eminem (who is a Caucasian) and Lotto (who is not), trading insults—or, rather, mixing a few insults with a generous measure of self-praise for being a superior "gangsta." Each criticizes the other's musical abilities, and in this case Lotto accuses Eminem of being a fraud—he is, after all, a young white man and not a "brother." There is a considerable amount of foul language in their exchange, but it is not very imaginative, as it doesn't go much farther than "shit" and "fuck." More striking, however, is the fact that there is no "call-and-response" back and forth. One goes on for about two dozen lines of rapping, and the other answers with another two dozen lines. And most striking of all is the absence of "Yo' Mama," except at the very end of Eminem's rap, when he says,

> My motto, fuck Lotto
> I'll get them digits [recordings] from your mother for a dollar
> tomorrow

Eminem was involved in battle rap offscreen, too, most memorably, perhaps, in his exchange with Benzino, another rapper who also happened to be co-owner of the *Source*, a magazine in which he published ratings for rap CDs. Eminem's complaint against Benzino was that the *Source* had awarded his *Marshall Mathers LP* only two stars, while others' recordings (Tupac Shakur and Jay Z, for instance) were routinely awarded four, the highest possible. Benzino's response to Eminem's complaints came in his "Pull Your Skirt Up":

> Let me start from the beginning, you ain't reppin' the streets
> You from the outskirts of Detroit, where the bitches meet
> I'm gonna pull your skirt up, expose your true sex
> Antagonize your label, till I get my respect
> . . . Don't let me have to backslap your moms if you smile
> I'm serious, if you ain't gon' respect her why should I?

And, toward the end of the number (which goes on for two single-spaced pages),

> I think we both know exactly what we here for
> I want the streets back, I'm coming to your door
> I earn my stripes
> I'm a don
> You a pussy
> Zino bombs hit you out the park
> You still a rookie

Eminem's answer came in his "Nail in the Coffin," which begins,

> I would never claim to be no Ray Benzino
> An 83-year-old fake pacheno

And ends with,

> I don't need your little fucking magazine
> I got double-XL's number anyways,
> And y'all can't stand it cause they gettin' bigger than y'all
> Oh, and by the way, how did I look at the VMAS
> When you was watchin' me from whatever TV you was watching
> from
> In Boston, the mean streets of Boston
> Fucking sissy
> And you gotta stand up you mutha fucker
> Suck my mutha fuckin' dick
> Oh, and for those that don't know
> Don't get it twisted
> The *Source* has a white owner!

A little exegesis may be in order. "Reppin'" means "representing," i.e., being a true example of a streetwise gangsta. "Pacheno" is a reference to Al Pacino's role in *The Godfather* and is a direct response to Benzino's "I'm a don"—i.e., a high-level gangster. "Double-XL" is another rap magazine, *XXL*. "VMAs" refers to a music awards show.

What is clear here are the conflicting claims of masculinity, talent, and reputation. Notice, too, the appearance of some of the traditional invective loci: origins (Boston vs. Detroit), sexual practices and orientation, cowardice, hypocrisy, and the like. Predictable insults, to be sure. But, as with the scene from *8 Mile*, we are far from the dozens. However much some might want to see the dozens behind such exchanges as these, we must remember that there is ample room for insults without the dozens. And besides, "Yo' mama" is conspicuously absent.

Mind Your Manners

We earlier commented on the fact that certain gestures are interpreted differently in other cultural settings—the "thumbs up," for instance. But other behaviors are likewise inoffensive in one culture, insulting in another. Maintaining eye contact during a conversation or meeting is expected in the U.S., for instance. But Chinese are taught to avoid eye contact, particularly when in the company of someone of higher social status. Indeed, it is not uncommon to see Asians close their eyes when someone is speaking to them, which in the U.S. would likely be interpreted as a sign of boredom or lack of interest. In Japan, however, it is a way of avoiding visual distraction, enabling the listener to concentrate only on what is being said. It is customary in the U.S., and so expected, that, on meeting someone for the first time, one should introduce oneself. In Japan, this is perceived as an aggressive gesture, and it is expected that one would wait to be introduced by someone else.

Asian dining etiquette is also different from Western. Typically, people dining in an American or European restaurant will order their own meals, intending them to be only for themselves. Chinese more often order a number of dishes, which are put in the middle of the table for all to share. At a Chinese dinner table, it is considered an omen of bad luck to flip a fish on a plate from one side to the other. It is also considered bad manners to finish all the food on one's plate, as that is perceived as a sign of disrespect for the host; and one must be careful not to rest one's chopsticks on a bowl or plate so that they point directly at someone.

It is not just Asian customs that need to be understood in order to avoid possible insults, of course. In Germany or France, the misuse of pronouns—failing to distinguish between the formal and familiar forms of second-person pronouns—can lead to faux pas. On the other hand, punctuality is treated very casually by the French, whereas in the U.S., tardiness is seen as rude. As cuisine is traditionally considered very important by the French, the rules of dining etiquette are strictly observed. One of them is that guests are expected to arrive with a gift—flowers, for example. If one wants to bring wine or a dessert, it should be arranged beforehand with the host to make sure it complements the main course. Smoking or drinking hard liquor before a meal are frowned upon, as they compromise the tastebuds, suggesting that the diner is not much interested in what is served.

Such are the norms of polite society, and not just in France. But it was not always so, evidently. In the 1997 motion picture *Ridicule*, directed by Patrice Leconte, we see another side of French "polite society." The movie is set in 1783, when (as the movie's epigram puts it) "Wit [*esprit*] was still king," and it tells the story of a young hydraulic engineer, Grégoire Ponceludon, who works his way into and up in the court of Louis XVI at Versailles in his efforts to secure support for a drainage project in his impoverished home district. A sympathetic nobleman, the Marquis de Bellegarde, counsels him: "Be witty and malicious and you'll succeed." And indeed, it turns out that wit, as measured by the cleverness of one's insults, is the key to recognition and acceptance.

In his encounters with the Versailles courtiers, Grégoire shows that he is capable of holding his own. He wanders into a room where a game of dominos is in progress, and he is told that there is a fee for joining in the game. One of the players, the Abbé de Villencourt, says to him, "You must find the ways of the court at Versailles very strange," and Grégoire replies, "Judge not lest you be judged." He explains that the only thing of value he has are the buckles on his shoes, and when the Abbé looks down to examine them, he adds, "You'll judge their worth better by bowing lower." Bellegarde and his daughter, Mathilde (who has read Pascal), give Grégoire lessons on how to dress and comport himself: "Don't laugh with your mouth open. It's coarse." But it is Grégoire's native *esprit* that guarantees his successes.

At a dinner party given by the Count Ballencourt, a would-be noble and academicien claims to be a distant relation of Ballencourt and points to a portrait of Ballencourt's grandfather, depicted on horseback, drawing attention to his resemblance to their "common ancestor." Grégoire remarks, to the delight of the others at the table, "He's the one with four legs." When the aspiring academicien, who claims to be the Baron de Gueret, commits a grammatical error, the Abbé observes, "Every harem has its eunuch." Not long after, the "Baron" hangs himself.

But Grégoire continues to succeed. At another dinner, the evening's entertainment consists of a competition in which the contestants are asked to produce, ex tempore, metrical epigrams. "A dull epigram," Bellegarde warns Grégoire, "will count against you." The Abbé comes up with one in iambics, but Grégoire prevails with his, in octosyllabics. At yet another dinner, a dinner for "wits"—one of whom announces, "I no longer consort with whores. They're as depraved as gentlewomen"— Grégoire responds to an insult directed at him by one Chevernoy with "The ass[hole] is wider than the mouth," and this results in a duel with Chevernoy in which Grégoire kills him. This proves to be too much for Grégoire to bear, and he returns home, empty-handed.

A voice in the background intones,

> Wit debonair in the
>   Age of Voltaire
> Was seen as a heaven-sent
>   treasure.
> Wit opened doors
>   to the company of Lords
> and the tasting of noble pleasures.
> In the past it was able
>   to put food on the table,
> but those days are gone forever.

Given this hasty summary of *Ridicule*, it may be hard to see how we can talk about etiquette in a setting where dinner is looked upon as a contact sport. If etiquette is thought of as observance of the proprieties of rank and occasion, we must wonder at the sense the movie's characters have of what is "proper." But if we bear in mind that, in French, *etiquette* also means "label" or "ticket," it makes rather more sense to look upon their ways of making a good impression as an exercise in etiquette: insults as the ticket to social rank.

Insults as "Rhetoric"

While this book is not intended to make its readers better at insults, nevertheless, looking back at the examples we have just surveyed, a number of basic recommendations for the would-be insulter emerge. First, "Know thine enemy." You want to be sure you're insulting the one you mean to insult, as Falstaff clearly failed to do with Master Ford. You also want to find out what your target's sore points are. Cicero's attack on Piso was particularly nasty since Piso sought for years to project an image of upright Roman manly virtue. And if there is a third-party audience present—the senate, or a group gathered around two contestants doing the dozens—make sure they share the set of beliefs and values you are explicitly or implicitly claiming to represent. You obviously want them on your side, not on your opponent's.

Second, be coherent. As we saw, using the Shakespeare Insult Kit without forethought can result not in a Shakespearean insult, but in nonsense; and the insults by *Monty Python's* Butcher and French Guard are too laughable—"Your father smelt of elderberries," indeed—to be appreciated as genuine insults. Along with this, avoid "I" statements: the intended insult is not about you, but about your opponent. Stick to the program. This is something Benzino and Eminem seem to have missed, and the result is mere adolescent boasting.

Third, it is probably not a coincidence that the invective loci we saw in Cicero reappear regularly in different eras and genres. After all, Cicero and Shakespeare and Monty Python are all part of the same cultural tradition. And it is, after all, hard to think of "topics" for insults that add significantly to our list. So the list is worth bearing in mind as a resource. More important, perhaps, is the ability to say (or write) the same thing in different ways. There is a verbal arsenal for insults in English, French, Polish—indeed, in any language—that is available to anyone who cares to think about it. Once again, it is surprising that students asked to compile a list of terms of abuse find it so hard to do. And one is reminded, once again, of the relative poverty of the insults thrown out during rap beefs—at least as compared (if it is fair to do so) to Martial or Shakespeare. Bear in mind that the language of insult is not a collection of intrinsically abusive terms.

Fourth, avail yourself of devices designed to provide your insult with a punchline. Merely hurling one-liners or epithets is seldom very effective. We saw in Martial and in Shakespeare some excellent examples of "artful" insults. Mastery of such devices comes, again, with practice.

In short, pay attention to situation, vehicle, and intensity, the three fundamental dimensions we sketched out at the very beginning. Insult fluency does not come easily, but can be attained through continued practice.

Not surprisingly, perhaps, our recommendations also cover ground laid out in traditional Greco-Roman rhetorics. Attention to situation and audience and the implementation of invective loci fit easily into the traditional canons of invention. Constructing insults with punchlines—i.e., guaranteeing intensity—falls under *dispositio*, or arrangement. It also falls under *elocutio*, or expression, as does the mastery of the lexicon of insults in your language of choice. And running mentally through the loci is not only part of inventing an insult—it also requires a good memory.

What of delivery? Only one of our examples seems to be pertinent there: the witty (and hardly rehearsed) exchanges in *Ridicule*. On the other hand, what is missing in written rhetoric, the *actio* of traditional rhetoric, is supplied by the tropes and figures we saw in many of our examples: repetition, hyperbole, exclamations, rhetorical questions, pleonasm, ellipsis, and the rest.

So, without trying very hard, it is possible to conceive of insults as fitting into the traditional discipline of rhetoric. But, on the one hand, the ancients discovered that long ago; and, on the other, fitting insult into those traditional categories seems hardly worth spending much time on, in any event. Certainly, no such formalist exercise can teach us what we really need to know: how to size up a situation. And, as we know, situation is everything.

CHAPTER 3

Beyond "Traditional" Rhetoric

Our examples exhibit a number of features common to traditional rhetorics. To name just a few, we note the repeated appearance of loci and the frequent appearance of traditional lines of argument. Here and there, we see the tactical use of humor and the deliberate construction of authoritative character. We see artful composition at every level, from the smallest units to larger compositions, both verbal and visual. We see tropes and figures in material as varied as formal speeches and the dozens. But, clearly, we are not seeing "rhetoric" as it is traditionally conceived: as a unilateral mode of gaining compliance or belief, usually by means of tactics involving some combination of argument and ingratiation. An art of insult is surely not an art of persuasion, as commonly understood. So perhaps we need to approach our subject from some different angles.

The Paradox of Insult

The conduct of Monty Python's Butcher and French Guards is clearly meant to be abusive, even if it is true that the customer in the butcher shop doesn't seem to feel abused (Arthur's knights are a different matter). And consider what Cicero does to Antony, for instance, or Grégoire to Chevernoy or, in one of the more sordid episodes of battle rap, Tupac Shakur to Biggie Smalls. And recall the consequences: the beheading and mutilation of Cicero, the duel in which Chevernoy is killed, and the murder of Biggie Small after a party in Los Angeles. It is not clear that the last of these was fundamentally a response to insults (there were gang-related and drug-related factors, as well), but evidently those who felt insulted (with very good reason) retaliated with murderous intent.

But why was Antony insulted when Cicero accused him of being a drunkard and a catamite? Looked at one way, we might say that it is only natural that one who has been injured seeks revenge. But looked at another, might we not say that Antony and Cicero shared the same opinion of drunkards and catamites? That is, beneath their enmity there is a substratum of agreement? And the same can be said about Eminem and Benzino and about those who do the dozens regarding manliness and wealth. What, then, about racial or ethnic slurs? What sort of "identification" plays out when one person calls another a "nigger" or a "kike"? It's hard to see how that is not meant to injure. But in such cases both the insulter and the insulted share the knowledge of what associations such terms of abuse are intended to call up: lowly, servile, dirty, uneducated, physically and sexually threatening less-than-human beings, for instance, and both parties probably share the same feelings toward such beings—i.e., there is an intimate sharing of both beliefs and values here. The Chinese host who is insulted when a Westerner places his chopsticks improperly is a different case, for the Westerner does so in ignorance and thus unintentionally insults his host. But the host does not recognize that, as "ignorance of the law is no excuse." Here we should say simply that there was a communication breakdown, a faulty interpretation of the situation. (The notion of an "intimate sharing" between insulter and insulted, one might argue, may help explain the complicity of the *Judenräte* [Jewish Councils] appointed by the Nazis as part of their plan to eliminate the maximum number of Jews with the least possible administrative effort and cost.)

The ability of an insulter to enlist the support of an audience works in a similar fashion. Martial articulates the public morality of the Roman upper class and points it at "someone" (as most of the objects of Martial's scorn turn out to be fictional characters) who fails to measure up to those ethical norms. Shakespeare communicates to his audience of Londoners his negative feelings toward obtuse lawyers and Welshmen, thus bringing to his audience's mind feelings they share with one another. The authors and distributors of *Flugschriften* seek to consolidate their audience's "us against them" stance by repeating what "everybody knows": that the pope is a pervert, and priests steal and are little more than pernicious beasts. Yea saying by nay saying. So all of these are modalities not of opposition and division, but of what Kenneth Burke called "identification," one of the foundational principles of his *Rhetoric of Motives*.

The Economics of Shame

Many of the observations about shame that Aristotle makes in his *Rhetoric* (2.6, 1383b12–1385a15) have a bearing on the subject of insults. In the chapter devoted to shame, he discusses the causes of shame, those before whom people feel shame, and the state of mind of those who feel shame—this distribution of subjects being systematic, not just arbitrary. This is probably not the place to provide a close reading of *Rhetoric* 2.6, but one of the general points Aristotle seems to make is that shame is most likely to be felt in social settings that attach importance to honor. Shame is felt in societies where, as we noted in connection with Cicero's speeches, reputation matters a great deal, where the opinions of others are valued, where honor can be attained or lost, where social rank is of significance, where credit can be extended and debts owed, where there are fragile bonds of intimacy, and where prestige can be measured by one's good looks, family ties, wealth, and knowledge. Aristotle is of course thinking of the Greek—specifically, perhaps, Athenian—social institutions of his age. But the obvious intersections with the invective loci that seem to show up in areas as diverse as Martial's epigrams and the dozens—and even in battle rap— suggest that his observations continue to be in play. Stupidity, poverty, ugliness, and suspect family ties are, after all, things to be ashamed of, and so one who is accused of being illegitimate, ugly, poor, and stupid—or, for that matter, a drunkard and a glutton—is likely to feel insulted, i.e., dishonored.

The problem is that there is only a limited supply of honor and reputation to go around, and a high demand. One cannot choose one's "Mama" or one's race, but one can (at least in theory) better one's standing in the community by acquiring wealth or education or by buying a new suit in the latest high fashion. So there is a scramble for a piece of the action everywhere one looks, whether in Detroit or Khartoum or Versailles. There are, of course, value differentiations in different situations. *Ridicule* shows how, in the court of Louis XVI, displays of *esprit* can overcome shortcomings in one's lineage, or even one's pocketbook.

In many cultures, value is assigned automatically—sons, for instance, being valued more than daughters. But what happens then is that all the sons are in a scramble to see who is the best son, and the same is true among the daughters. The short supply of reputation, in other words, may explain the ubiquity of insults.

But we can't reduce the social economies of insult to simple matters of supply and demand. In a related passage in the *Rhetoric*, in the chapter on anger (2.2), Aristotle has this to say about "slighting" (*oligôria*):

> Slighting is the actively entertained opinion that something is obviously of no importance . . . You feel contempt for what you consider unimportant, and that is the sort of thing that you slight . . . The person who gives insult also belittles, for insult is doing or speaking in which there is shame to the sufferer, not that some advantage may accrue to you or because something happened to you, but simply for the pleasure involved. . . . The cause of the pleasure thus enjoyed is that [the insulter] thinks himself greatly superior to others when illtreating them. That is why the young and the rich are given to insults; for by insulting they think they are superior. (1378b10–28)

In this case, I will take the liberty of offering a few observations about detail. The word I have translated "insult" is the Greek *hybris*; but this *hybris* is not "the o'erweening pride" of Aristotle's tragic hero in the *Poetics*. It is a technical term in Athenian law that refers to any assault, private or public, by word or action, on the integrity of another—of another citizen, that is. It was an actionable offense. Accordingly, I prefer (as does George Kennedy in his admirable translation of the *Rhetoric*) "doing or speaking" to the reading found in most manuscripts at 1378b23, "*blaptein kai lupein*," which would translate as "harming and distressing," both of which an act of *hybris* would presumably do. Secondly, I would, in view of what I have said about "the scramble," take issue with Aristotle's "simply for the pleasure involved."

But I think Aristotle has it right: insulters arrogate to themselves a superiority to those whom they insult. Whether they are really superior (as a rich man to a poor) or merely think they are superior, insulters identify themselves with a higher moral or social status (they are not, of course, the same thing) and their targets with a lower. Clearly, this is what Cicero did (among other things) in the cases involving Catiline, Piso, and Antony. And it is also what the authors and distributors of the *Flugschriften* (on both sides) were up to. They were not simply trying to consolidate their supporters. They were trying to persuade them that they were morally superior to the other side, which they achieved, in part, by the animal imagery we saw in the accompanying engravings, for instance. It was by asserting their moral superiority that they were able to consolidate their support. And we must remember that the audiences of the religious pamphlets often included members of the lower social classes; whereas the opposition—at least in the Reformation literature—was seen as rotten with luxury.

In the case of Martial, things work a little differently. Martial's readers were invited to identify with him—as both a moral authority and a skillful poet—so as to get them to identify (more actively, perhaps) with the basis of his moral authority, traditional Roman virtues. Except in a few cases, it will be recalled, the "opposition" was fictional, not actual—an abstraction at best of "the worst." So in Martial's case, it might be said that identification was prior to the establishment of their position in the moral hierarchy. And in the case of Al Capp, we have another variation, as Capp invited shifting and inverted identifications to show that the "superior" class is not as superior as it might think.

Maintaining vs. Interrogating Hierarchies

In talking about the use of insults to achieve "identification" and to successfully compete for status in an economy of scarcity, we are talking about the tactical uses of insult. I'd like to propose some further reflections on tactics and the goals they are designed to achieve. This will require bringing in some more examples that bring out a little more clearly some of the subtleties and tensions that emerge when we look more closely at the hierarchical dimension of insult.

In 1938, *Kampf dem Weltfeind* (*War against the World Enemy*), a collection of speeches by Julius Streicher, one of the architects of Nazi policies regarding the Jews, appeared in German bookstores. This collection, published by *Der Stürmer* (which was controlled by Streicher), contains thirty-three speeches given between 1920 and 1933. The content of these speeches is fairly predictable, with echoes and amplifications of material in Hitler's *Mein Kampf* and a great deal of shabby "anthropology." While we don't find there some of the old commonplaces of anti-

Semitism, such as the notorious "blood libel" (that rabbis kidnapped Christian children and used their blood to make matzos), we find the usual assertions that Jews are to be both despised and feared. They have no culture, or even language, of their own; they are ugly; they are an insidious foreign influence, polluting the purity of the German *Volk*; they have no honest trades; are interested only in money; and as a result, they work behind the scenes to undermine the German economy as well as its culture—in short, many of the charges brought up in *The Protocols of the Elders of Zion* (from which Streicher quotes in a 1929 Munich speech, 115).

The *Protocols*, first published in Russia in 1905 and translated soon thereafter into a dozen languages (including English), portrayed Jews as diabolical schemers, financiers plotting world domination. This hoax, alas, is still with us, being particularly popular recently with certain Arab Islamicists. It was written in 1898 by a Russian expatriate, Mathieu Govolinski, who used as his sources an antiroyalist pamphlet from 1864 (against Napoleon III, entitled "A Dialogue in Hell between Montaigne and Machiavelli," with "Machiavelli's" words put in the mouths of conspiratorial Jews) and an 1868 German novel, *Biarritz*, by Hermann Goedsche (which describes a nocturnal meeting of rabbis in a Prague cemetery, laying perfidious plans). Hitler was introduced to it by the Nazi ideologue Alfred Rosenberg, and he cites it innumerable times in *Mein Kampf*. The Nazi party saw to the publication of two dozen German editions during the 1920s and 1930s. By the outbreak of hostilities in 1939, accordingly, it had become "what everyone knows"—or, at least, what every intelligent German "knew."

Streicher does more, of course, than simply paraphrase the *Protocols*. He repeatedly celebrates the successes of Hitler (as in a 1926 Munich "man of the hour" speech) and charges the Jews with being Bolsheviks (in a May 1928 Nürnberg address); threatening German womanhood (in a Christmas 1925 Nürnberg speech, 61), "quoting" the Talmud (56); and being responsible for the "early death" of a fellow Nazi (one Heinrich Wölfel). All of this will prepare Germany for the "Final Solution": the elimination of the inferior Jews as both permissible and necessary for the survival of the Master Race.

Meanwhile, at about the same time (after 1920), similar claims were appearing in a newspaper published in Dearborn, Michigan, home of the corporate headquarters of Ford Motor, the *Dearborn Independent*. The man behind the *Dearborn Independent* was none other than Henry Ford, who had bought it when it had fallen on hard times and hired writers (who claimed no bylines) to disseminate his anti-Semitic ideas: Jews were responsible for the Great War, for instance, and much, much more (as we shall see). Ford required every Ford dealership in the country to display copies, and the paper's editors (who are nowhere named) published collections of *Independent* editorials in book form for distribution nationwide. (The quotations in what follows are from *The International Jew: The World's Foremost Problem*, vol. 3, *Jewish Influences in American Life*, and vol. 4, *Aspects of Jewish Power in the United States*.)

It is hard to know where to begin. In "Candid Address to Jews on the Jewish Problem" (editorial of January 7, 1922), the editors write,

> It is true that beneath all the network of trivializing influences in literature, art, politics, economics, fashion and sport, is Jewish influence controlled by Jewish groups. Their Orientalism has served as a subtle poison to dry up the sound serum of Anglo-Saxon morality on which this country thrived in its formative years. Is it necessary to specify? In every movement toward a lower standard, a looser relationship, especially toward the overthrow of the old Christian safeguards, do not Jewish names predominate? (4:225)

In a single editorial, from May 1921, "Angles of Jewish Influence in American Life," we read that what sets the Jew apart is the fact that he is not interested in "making" money, only "getting" it.

> It is the "geld" that counts. He has no attachment for the things he makes, for he doesn't make any; he deals in the things which other men make and regards them solely on the side of their money-drawing value. "The joy of creative labor" is nothing to him, not even an intelligible saying. (4:43)

Jews are responsible for Communist influence in American colleges and for the infiltration of the American labor movement by "foreign . . . alien, destructive and treasonable" elements (44). Jews are responsible, too, for the "flaccid condition of the Church" by their promotion of "Jewish-German higher criticism" (45–46)—this on top of the other threats from "rampant Socialism and Sovietism" (46). "Into the camp of [the Anglo-Saxon] race," they write,

among the sons of the rulers, comes a people that has no civilization to point to, no aspiring religion, no universal speech, no great
achievement in any realm but the realm of "get," cast out of every
land that gave them hospitality, and these people endeavor to tell the
sons of the Saxons what is needed to make the world what it ought
to be. (51)

And it gets much worse than that:

Jews are not sportsmen. This is not set down in complaint against
them, but merely an analysis. It may be a defect in their character,
or it may not; it is nevertheless a fact which discriminating Jews un-
hesitatingly acknowledge. Whether this is due to their physical leth-
argy, their dislike of unnecessary physical action, or their serious cast
of mind, others may decide; the Jew is not naturally an out-of-door
sportsman. (38)

This is from "Jewish Gamblers Corrupt American Baseball" (Septem-
ber 3, 1921, 3:27–50). Not being inclined to exercise, and forever interested in the "get," they "set out to capitalize rivalry and commercialize
contestant zeal" (39). And the result is:

When you contrast the grand stands full of Americans supposing
they are witnessing "the only clean sport," with the sinister groups
playing with the players and managers to introduce a serpent's trail
of unnecessary crookedness, you get a contrast that is rather star-
tling. And the sinister influence is Jewish. (50)

The "crookedness" they refer to is exemplified by the infamous "Black
Sox Scandal," the result of the Chicago White Sox "throwing" the 1919
World Series, due to the "sinister influence" of Jewish gamblers—who
are also, by the way, responsible for contemporary rowdyism at baseball games.

[T]he rowdyism that has afflicted baseball, especially in the East, is
all of Jewish origin—the razzing of the umpires, hurling of bottles,
ceaseless shouting of profanities. ("Jewish Degradation of American
Baseball," 3:51)

In "Jewish Jazz Becomes Our National Music" (3:64–74), we read,

Jazz is a Jewish creation. The mush, the slush, the sly suggestion, the abandoned sensuousness of sliding notes, are of Jewish origin. Monkey talk, jungle squeals, grunts and squeaks and gasps suggestive of cave love are camouflaged by a few feverish notes and admitted to homes where the thing itself, unaided by the piano, would be stamped out in horror. (3:65)

The Jew is everywhere. Jews were behind the treason of Benedict Arnold (see 4:67–99); Jews control Tammany Hall (fooling the Irish, who think they are in control, 3:141–66); they manipulate the Federal Reserve Plan (3:205–16); have made American labor unions "hot-beds of Bolshevism" (3:88–100); and, as one comes to expect, are responsible for "America's money famine" (3:243–56).

The Jewish program to control and "get" from the American economy is, according to the *Independent*, well known. In "The Economic Plans of International Jews" (July 1922; 4:193–206), the evidence is laid out. "It will be worth while," they say, ". . . to recall some of the forecasts and plans made in these most remarkable documents which have been attributed to the Wise Men of Zion, the world leaders of the inner council" (4:195)—that is, *The Protocols of the Elders of Zion*, quotations from and commentary on which make up most of the "story."

And in case the position of the *Dearborn Independent* is not completely clear, we find, toward the end of "Angles of Jewish Influence," the following:

> Let the heritage of our Anglo-Saxon-Celtic fathers have free course among their Anglo-Saxon-Celtic sons, and the Jewish idea can never triumph over it, in university forum or in the marts of trade. The Jewish idea never triumphs until first the people over whom it triumphs are denied the nurture of their native culture . . . Judah has made the invasion. Let it come . . . Let college students and leaders of thought know that the objective is the regency of the ideas and the race that have built all the civilization we see and that promise all the civilization of the future; let them also know that the attacking force is Jewish. (4:53)

So Streicher and Ford are up to the same thing: using insults to maintain the hierarchy they recognize. Of course, there is no mention of a Final Solution in the *Dearborn Independent*, but neither is there in *Kampf dem Weltfeind*. And it must be allowed that Henry Ford was probably more interested in keeping Jews out of the country clubs and keeping unions—those "hot-beds of Bolshevism"—out of his factories than in smashing Jewish storefront windows or convicting Jews of alleged acts of arson. Nevertheless, what we are seeing in the performances of Streicher and the *Dearborn Independent* might be viewed as examples of assertions of superiority aimed at getting their respective audiences—which did not include Jews, of course—to identify with the "Nordic" or "Anglo-Saxon-Celtic" ideals.

But there is a sense in which they are interrogating hierarchy at the same time that they are maintaining it. In both the German and American versions, anti-Semitism is defended by the claim that Jews exercise enormous influence on and control, in ways almost unimaginable, our daily lives. So they must, it seems, be despised; but they must also be feared. Hence, the rhetoric of denigration is an indirect means of questioning the legitimacy—in both the legalistic and psychological senses—of the implied hierarchy that puts the Jews in a superior position. In this respect, we can see another intersection with the *Flugschriften* we looked at earlier: on the one hand, Catholics are depicted as morally corrupt and as less than human, i.e., inferior. But they are also identified with the pope and the bishops and the nobility—the powerful; and the audience of the pamphlets, largely made up of lower-class and bourgeois "readers" is invited to question the legitimacy of that social and religious arrangement. And the invitation was accepted. And just as the peasants' revolts in the 1520s resulted in political upheavals, and Calvin was able to rewrite the ordinances of Geneva, so the Nazis enacted racial laws that denied citizenship and property rights to the Jews in the 1930s.

If these are examples of how the "superior" party puts down the "inferior," there is another tactic by which the "inferior" party more directly interrogates the existing hierarchy and, by doing so, shows it to be despicable. A good example of this tactical use of insults can be seen in Aristophanes' *Knights*, produced in Athens in 424 BCE. I do not intend to go into great detail about this play—a play that has given scholars some major headaches—but want to concentrate on how Aristophanes frames his critique of the politicians that ran Athens at the time.

The play consists in great part of a competition between Paphlagon and the Sausage-seller for the favors of Demos (the People), who is depicted early in the play as a shabby and somewhat senile old man. In the end, the Sausage-seller prevails, rejuvenates old Demos, and the two of them go off in triumph together. It is hard to see in the play a consistent political allegory, but one thing is clear: the intended target of Aristophanes' satire was Kleon, the leading politician in Athens at the time. Kleon is mentioned by name only once (in passing, by the chorus of the play, at v. 976), but there is ample internal evidence to make it clear that he is to be identified with Paphlagon.

Paphlagon is so named because he is allegedly of Paphlagonian ancestry (Paphlagonia, at the eastern limits of the known world, is like Al Capp's Slobbovia), and there is also a bit of wordplay on the Greek *paphlazein*, "to storm" or "to bluster"—i.e., a loudmouth. He is described in the opening scene of the play as a *panourgos*, "a complete scoundrel" (a term used a dozen times to describe him), a thief, a liar, a devious swindler, and a bribetaker. We elsewhere learn that he is by trade a dealer in hides, an embezzler, and the paragon of shamelessness (*anaideia*). And indeed, from his first entrance on, he exhibits just those characteristics.

In the course of the opening scene, two slaves (or houseboys) filch from the drunk and sleeping Paphlagon an oracle that reveals that Paphlagon is destined to be overthrown by a sausage-seller. And just as we learn that, the Sausage-seller makes his entrance (at 148). He is assured by one of the slaves that he is the ideal replacement for the current leader (Paphlagon), as he is "loudmouthed, low-class, and *thrasus*," which might best be translated as "a bust-out." And by his own account, he is also a thief, a slanderer, and given to bribery, too—an expert at stealing and lying. And he is proud of it.

And so the contest to see who will be favored by Demos comes down to which of the two, Paphlagon and the Sausage-seller, is worse. After a protracted series of competitions—from a slanging match to flattery, the production of false oracles, and gift-giving, the Sausage-seller is declared the winner by Demos. Demos is then rejuvenated by the Sausage-seller and is hailed by the chorus as *monarchos* and *basileus* ("king") of the Greeks (a rather odd acclamation in democratic Athens), and he promises to punish wrongdoers, pay the fleet, and keep teenagers out of the marketplace. Paphlagon is sent off in disgrace.

It is clear that Aristophanes has made use of the stock topics of invective in his construction of Paphlagon, the Sausage-seller (whose name, "Agorakritos," "Chosen of the Marketplace," we learn only at 1257), and, indeed, of Demos, who is called "mindless and senile" and is won over by flattery and gifts. The slanging match (see 272–98) resembles the battle rap we saw earlier. The way our expectations are shaped during the opening scene of the play reminds us of the "contracts" that Shakespeare made with his audience at the beginning of *Merry Wives of Windsor*. So, while watching *Knights*, we find ourselves in familiar territory.

But there are several aspects of this production that need to be borne in mind. The first is the way in which the characters in the play address the audience in the theatre directly. There was no "fourth wall" in Athenian drama. Added to this is the second aspect: Kleon himself, seated prominently in the first row, and all of the politicians—members of the assembly and its board of councilors—were there to see themselves lampooned. In *Knights*, it is the lower class—indeed, the lowest—that prevails against the ruling classes, all, evidently, for the good of the Demos, or the People. One lesson that the audience might have taken away is that Athenians must learn to see through the props and role playing of politicians who claim to love the city.

I do not think the play can be reduced to the sort of political allegory this implies. But it is clear, if this reading makes any sense, that we are dealing here with a rhetoric of interrogation, an invitation to think critically about what is going on in Athenian politics. And the chief vehicle Aristophanes uses to promote that critical thinking is insult, in this instance sanctioned insult. *Knights* was produced for the dramatic competition held during the festival of Lenaia, so called because it was originally held in the Lenaion precinct of Athens. The audience at the Lenaia was exclusively Athenian, unlike the better-known Dionysia, which was attended by envoys from all over Greece (and abroad, it seems). It was accordingly permitted to say things about local politics at the Lenaia that were not permitted during the Dionysia—or, at least, were liable to get a playwright in trouble if he did. This, if we can believe what was said in Aristophanes' *Acharnians*, produced at the Lenaia of 425 BCE, is what happened to Aristophanes, and at the hands of Kleon himself. At *Acharnians* 377ff., Dikaiopolis ("Mr. Just City," who here speaks for Aristophanes) says,

In my own case I know what Kleon did to me because of last year's comedy. He hauled me before the Council and slandered me, tongue-lashed me with lies, and roared like Cycloborus [an Attic stream], and soaked me [in abuse].

And a little later (at 502ff.):

For this time Kleon won't accuse me of
Abusing Athens when foreigners are here.
We're by ourselves; it's the Lenaia;
No foreigners are here yet.

Knights, then, may be seen as payback for Kleon's action, if it ever did in fact occur. It is certainly what seems to be a fulfillment of a promise made by the chorus in *Acharnians* at 299ff.: "I hate you even more than Kleon / whom I intend to cut up as shoe-leather for the knights."

Aristophanes, in short, was permitted to insult the city's leaders at the Lenaia. Indeed, he may have been expected to do that, not so much because (as some have suggested) the festival was a sort of *Carneval*, where the playwright/jester could say what he wanted with impunity, but because that was one of the festival's purposes: to provide a forum for interrogation of the prevailing hierarchy.

Knights, incidentally, won that year's prize for best comedy. And Kleon, also incidentally, was elected general the following year.

Insults directed at those higher in the hierarchy are certainly not limited to the Athenian Lenaia. Think, for instance, of Mark Twain's *The Gilded Age*, with its scathing portrayal of Washington politics, particularly the rank hypocrisy of Senator Dilworthy, "The Golden-tongued Statesman." But Twain's main tactic is not insult itself, but irony. For an example of more direct "insults from below," we have to look elsewhere. A good example can be found in J. C. Scaliger's attack on Erasmus.

Julius Caesar Scaliger (d. 1558), a transplanted Italian (his real name was Bordoni) practicing medicine in the small French town of Agen, decided to take on the famous Desiderius Erasmus, and published in Paris in 1531 his *Oratio pro M. Tullio Cicerone contra Erasmum*. The occasion for this was the publication in 1528 of Erasmus's *Ciceronianus*, a dialogue of sorts deriding the (mainly Italian) "Ciceronians" who insisted that Cicero's Latin was the only Latin that true humanists should imitate. So we have an instance in which an obscure physician in a backwater town takes it upon himself to defend that position against the criticisms of the Ciceronians whom Erasmus characterized as "apes" who had no regard for the central concept in true Ciceronian rhetoric, *decorum*— i.e., propriety regarding subject matter, time, and audience.

Scaliger's *Oratio* is a tour de force of invective. (References in what follows are to the line numbers in M. Magnien's magisterial edition in the series Travaux d'Humanisme et Renaissance, no. 329 [Geneva, 1999].) Erasmus, he says, is a slanderer and calumniator (14–17, 101, 131, 152, 634, 862, 1036, etc.), a vain liar (*vanus et mendax*, 266; see also 226, 725, 782, 847, etc.) motivated by envy (*livor*) (519, 878, 977, 988) and impudence (691, 1351, 1395, 1656). He is malicious beyond belief (948, 1513, 2166ff.) and evilly inclined (365, 615), but stupid (944, 1128, 1709) and half-educated (1222, 1354)—a real *rusticus* (777, 805, 1859, 1973) and a barbarian (218, 225, 816–22, 893). He is, after all, a Dutchman (486 [of "Teutons"], 630, 865, 904, 1342, 1464) with no appreciation of the finer (viz., Italian) things of life (e.g., 471–75, 775–81, 505–6, 1943–46) or of "Italian" eloquence (2182–84). Erasmus is a poisoner (146, 630, 826, 1413, 1594), a hatchetman (*carnifex*, 1529), a monster (822, 1519, 1638, 2131), a parricide (1530); but he is also a lapdog (*canicula*, 1888), an old crow (*anus cornicula*, 1275), and an old parrot (cf. *vetule psittace* at 656). What is more, he is a drunk (396, 472, 479, 501, 730, 804–15, 984), which explains why he made so many errors while working as a low-level (see "*semihomo*" at 805) proofreader at Aldo Manuzio's press in Venice. And most damning of all, he is antipope (311–15), a blasphemer (221–33, 1723–36), a deserter from the church (1681, 2179, 2204), a New Epicurean (1627) and admirer of Lucretius (1368–69), a promoter of the Reformation (1369–72) and of "the Pope of Basel" (309–15), i.e., an accomplice of Luther (756–57).

Although the purported audience is composed of students, the "*optimi adolescentes*" ("fine young men") addressed in the preface and frequently throughout (cf., e.g., 518, 794, 960, 976), Scaliger often addresses Erasmus himself: "*Erasme*" at 584, 737, 849, 1476, 1498, 1516, etc.; "*Batave*" ("Dutchman") at 630, 865, 904, 1464, etc.; and often with epithets—"*O monstrum*" (822), "*O insane*" (995), "*O disertissime calumniator*" (1235), "*O nequam*" ("O Mr. Nobody") (1513), "*O carnifex*" (1529), "*O rustice*" (1859). Scaliger also peppers his Erasmus with hostile questions (much as Luther did in his debate with Erasmus over free will), exhibiting deep hostility, as at, e.g., the run of questions at 986–95 or those at 1104–16, 1250–64, 1624–36, and 1739–48; or questions mixed with exclamations, as at 408–16 or 1393–1401.

A few examples may be in order, just to give a general idea of Scaliger's tone. At 390–96, for instance, we read:

> *O impurum hominem qui ea damnat, quae legibus prodita, quae censurissunt constituta, quae cum ipsa natura ab exordiis crescentis mundi coaluisse videmus. O nefandum qui quod Dominus Deusque noster egit infando improbitatis titulo circumfert. O vanum qui quod ipse agit alii vitio vertit. Quis te usquam amarulentior? Quas tu religiones insectatus non es? Quorum hominum ordines non lacerasti? Quibus tu Manibus bellum non indixisti? Quibus cum larvis temulente luctatus non es?*

[O vile man who condemns what the laws have promulgated, what the critics have decided, what we see since the very creation of the world, in harmony with Nature herself! O vile one, who spreads gossip about the acts of Our Lord God with unspeakable effrontery! O imposter who reproaches others for doing just what he does! Who has ever been more disagreeable than you? What religious orders have you not attacked? What classes of men have you not slandered? Against what spirits of the departed have you not declared war? With what specters have you not wrestled in your drunkenness?]

Or take what he says at 822–27:

> *O monstrum! Quo enim te alio appellem nomine, qui rerum naturam confundis? Si tu recte loqueris, atque id Ciceroni in primis debes, quid alios deterrebas? Si eo te fortuna impulit, voluntas exercuit, livor confirmavit, ut purissimos fontes haustos pro tua libidine lutosissimo veneno contaminares, corrumperes, quare vis in eodem haerere coeno studiosos?*

[Monster! (For what other name can I give to one who stirs up disorder in Nature?) If you speak well, you owe it all to Cicero, so why have you led others astray? If your way of life has compelled you, your will carried you away, if envy encouraged you to contaminate and spoil with the filthiest of poisons the source from which you derive such pleasure, why do you want to immerse students in the same filth?]

There is no question that Scaliger has learned the lessons taught by, say, Cicero's *Philippics* well. But why such vehement vituperation? It is tempting to answer by appealing to the very envy (*livor*) he accuses Erasmus of being encouraged by. Scaliger was in his forties when he composed this *oratio*, claimed to be of a noble family and to have studied with some of the most prestigious scholars in Italy—and yet there he was, practicing medicine in a small town far from Paris—even farther from Bologna or Florence—unknown to any of the luminaries of humanism in France or anywhere else. His attack on Erasmus, possibly the best-known intellectual in Europe at the time, was Scaliger's attempt to gain an entrée into the upper ranks of the *res publica litteraria*. His plan was to get his oration published and circulated among students in the colleges of Paris, as well as among working scholars in France, Italy, and England, by exposing the shortcomings of the *Ciceronianus* and taking up the cause of the ardent followers of Cicero himself.

In any event, once he was able to produce fair copy of his *Oratio*, he sent it with an emissary to Paris, where it was to be distributed among the students of the Collège de Navarre, where he thought the "*optimi adolescentes*" there would be swept away by his eloquence. Quite the contrary, as Scaliger would soon learn, the only thing swept away was the manuscript itself. Scaliger made a second attempt, this time successfully getting it into the hands of Pierre Vidou, a respected Paris printer, and the *Oratio* finally appeared in print.

It is unclear what Vidou's print run was, but evidently not many copies of the *Oratio* survived the hostile reception it received. For Erasmus's part, he did not see it until his friend Amerbach sent him a copy later in 1531. And as far as Erasmus was concerned, it was an attack by one of his old enemies, Girolamo Aleandro, who, Erasmus was convinced, used "Julius Caesar Scaliger" as a nom de plume. For reasons that scholars are still debating, Erasmus did not bother to respond to Scaliger's *Oratio*, although he did express his irritation at what he considered a slanderous pack of lies. In short, Scaliger's *Oratio* did not succeed in establishing his reputation as a courageous scholar unafraid to take on Europe's best-known humanist and gaining him a place among the elite of the literary world.

There is more to this story than we can tell here. But the main reason for bringing Scaliger into our discussion is that his *Oratio* is a good example of the use of insults for purposes of upward social mobility that we saw in our remarks on *Ridicule*. Seen thus in terms of the vertical axis of insult that we mentioned at the beginning of this book—that is, in terms of hierarchy—the *Oratio* can also be compared to Aristophanes' *Knights* in that it represents insults delivered by the lower-status party against the upper. And both of them can, in turn, be seen as complements to Streicher and Ford, whose insults against the Jews are meant to establish and maintain their position as superior (with all the paradoxes that come with anti-Semitism).

Enforcing "Civility"

At a White House reception held for senators-elect in 2006, President George W. Bush, it was reported, asked about the welfare of the son of James Webb, newly elected senator from Virginia. Webb's son, as it happens, was currently serving with the U.S. Marines in Iraq. Webb replied, "They [i.e., the troops] should come back now." "That's not what I asked," Bush said. And Webb's rejoinder was, "That's between me and my son." Conservative pundits were shocked by this exchange. How could Webb be so impolite? After all, the president is the president and should not be spoken to that way. How uncivil of Webb!

Such sensitivity to transgressions of civility seems more and more common lately, in spite of the fact that from one point of view it was Bush, and not Webb, who was uncivil. In other words, it is not only Bush's supporters who are sensitive. Television viewers are reported to object more frequently to comedians whose stock in trade includes ethnic or racial stereotypes. On college campuses, there are announcements of "codes of conduct" that include injunctions to "respect diversity" and forbid "hate speech." In the United Kingdom, Conservatives have called for laws (which seem to be aimed mainly at preachers in British mosques) against speech that is perceived as encouraging terrorism. Parents of children subjected to "cyberbullying"—being insulted via e-mails or Web sites—are calling for the enactment of child online protection laws to protect their children from emotional damage and lowered self-esteem.

It is not clear how passing laws forbidding "hate speech" would work, even in Britain, where they do not have a First Amendment guaranteeing freedom of speech to complicate things. Instead of working to "detoxify" terms of abuse (see our earlier discussion of "nigger"), some have turned to "codes of conduct" and legislation to restore civility to civic life. But, of course, who decides what constitutes "hate speech" or measures degrees of emotional damage? Most nations already have laws against libel; but those laws are generally hard to enforce. Libel cases, in any event, are civil cases, not criminal, and they always turn on the question of intent. We have already seen how complicated a matter that is. And why should insults by one individual addressed to another be against the law in the first place? But the final irony would be a situation that encourages litigation (of which there is no shortage already), which by nature is adversarial—hardly a recipe for the restoration of civility.

There are, of course, some laws on the books already that forbid "insults." In the course of an interview with a Swiss magazine in 2005, the Turkish novelist (and eventual Nobel laureate) Orhan Pamuk denounced the mass murder of Armenians by Ottoman forces during World War I and the killing of Kurds by Turks in the 1980s. For this, he was charged with a crime under a Turkish law (Article 301 of the penal code) against "insults to the Turkish nation." The case was eventually dismissed on a technicality in January 2006, but conviction would have resulted in serious prison time. Similarly, another Turkish novelist, Elif Shafak, was charged under the same provision in Turkish law. As it developed, it was not she who "insulted" the Turkish nation, but a character in one of her novels who made passing reference to genocide committed by Turks against Armenians. Her case, too, was dismissed. But the law—which should not be confused with laws against denying the Holocaust in France and Germany—is still in effect. Both cases, one might add, were widely protested and seen as undermining Turkish efforts to be admitted to the European Union. (Indeed, the suits against Pamuk and Shafak—and several others, including the editor of a bilingual Turkish-Armenian weekly newspaper, Hrant Dink, assassinated in Istanbul in January 2007—seem to be part of organized opposition to membership in the European Union. Responsible for those suits, and organizer of demonstrations timed to coincide with the resulting trials, is a right-wing attorney, Kemal Kerincsiz. Kerincsiz openly opposes membership and has acknowledged that such displays of Turkey's censorship laws aid his cause.)

And Turkey is not alone. In November 2006, the *New York Times* reported a debate in the Russian Duma on a proposed ban on criticizing one's opponents during an election campaign. In the wake of "free elections" in 2006, laws were enacted by the new assembly of Iraq that criminalize speech that ridicules the government or its officials (see the editorial in the *New York Times*, October 9, 2006). Any journalist, for instance, who "publicly insults" the government is subject to up to seven years in prison. About a dozen Iraqi journalists were charged with the crime of offending public officials. In one case, it is reported, a high school teacher was arrested after he wrote a letter to the editor in his local paper that party leaders in his area were acting "like pharaohs." Another reporter was charged with defamation when she quoted a protester comparing present-day Iraqi police with those of Sadaam Hussein. Other journalists were arrested for writing about a prominent official's dispute over a telephone bill. One would think the Iraqi government had other things to worry about.

We can also find instances of laws that apply to insults much closer to home than Turkey or Russia—notably, in some Southern states in the U.S. For instance, there was a Texas statute (repealed in the 1930s) that decreed that insulting words or actions directed toward a female constituted legal grounds for reducing a charge of murder to manslaughter. In North Carolina, it is considered libelous "to destroy the reputation of innocent and unprotected women, whose very existence in society depends upon the unsullied purity of their character," we are told by Charles P. Flynn (in *Insult and Society: Patterns of Comparative Interaction* [Port Washington, NY, 1977], 79). In Mississippi law, the use of expressions that are customarily understood as insults and "tend to breach the peace" are actionable. In 1900, 1905, and 1914, courts in Virginia, Louisiana, and South Carolina found the terms "colored" or "Negro" libelous when applied to a white man. And, of course, there is the (recently repealed) Texas "paramour law" (also, as I understand, part of the Napoleonic Code) that allowed a husband to kill his wife's lover if he caught them in flagrante delicto. But in American common law generally, no legal protection is accorded to someone who reacts violently to an insult, no matter how abusive, aggravating, contemptuous, false, grievous, indecent, insulting, opprobrious, provoking, or scurrilous the insult might be. The law rather requires one to walk away from another who is attempting to pick a fight.

Legislation against insults is probably against the free speech guarantees of the First Amendment, and it is almost certainly against another guarantee in that amendment, freedom of association. Insults, for instance, are a proven method of motivating military recruits and athletes to "shape up"—as any Marine drill instructor or football coach will tell you. And every year, thousands of young people aspiring to belong to a fraternity or sorority willingly subject themselves to humiliating hazing practices. They do so because they fervently desire to belong to the group, just as Marine recruits and football players desire to be "part of the team." Are exceptions to a law against insults to be made in those cases? Whether or not you have any desire to belong to such teams, why should those who do have such a desire be protected against threats to their self-esteem if, in fact, it is precisely self-esteem they are concerned with in wanting to join a team or a fraternity? Furthermore, it has long been recognized that insults are frequently the means to strengthen social bonds—recall what we said about the dozens. Charles Flynn quotes the following exchange between firefighters, as reported by Dennis Smith in his *Report from Engine 82* (New York, 1972):

> "Yessir, men, Mrs. O'Mann is cooking Irish footballs tonight, and she requests that you clean off the tables." Billy-o hears the remark, and approaches waving a long-pronged fork in his hand. "Listen, Charlie," he says, "I don't mind you calling me Mrs. O'Mann, just as long as you don't try to touch my body." "He doesn't need you, Billy-o," Jerry Herbert says, "because he can get his own Mrs. McCarthy for a deuce any time he wants."
> Everyone laughs . . . (83)

What Smith (and Flynn) is getting at is the way nonserious insults sustain a sense of comradeship, cultivating the kind of intimacy that, paradoxically, can go along with insulting behavior. So passing laws against insults not only threatens constitutional rights; doing so also threatens what Flynn calls "primary social relationships."

In short, given the combination of unsavory parallels and threats to the texture of social life, legislating against insults does not seem to be a very good idea.

The Aesthetic Angle

We find in Robert Schnakenberg's *Distory: A Treasury of Historical Insults* (New York, 2004) an item from *Harper's Magazine* calling Abraham Lincoln a "filthy storyteller, despot, liar, thief, braggart, buffoon, usurper, monster, ignoramus Abe, old scoundrel, perjurer, swindler, tyrant, field-butcher, land-pirate" (23). While this is rather more sophisticated than, for instance, what Eminem says to Benzino, it is scarcely more than name-calling—and shapeless name-calling, at that. By contrast to the "And I speak as a friend" insult we saw earlier, or to some of the epigrams of Martial, the *Harper's* example is artless in the extreme. And that brings us to another area of social relations, the aesthetic.

Consider the remark H. L. Mencken once made about Warren G. Harding (also in *Distory*, 39–40):

> He writes the worst English that I have ever encountered. It reminds me of a string of wet sponges; it reminds me of tattered washing on the line; it reminds me of stale bean soup, of dogs barking through endless nights. It is so bad that a sort of grandeur creeps into it. It drags itself out of the dark abyss of pish and crawls insanely up the topmost pinnacle of posh. It is flap and doodle. It is balder and dash.

Mencken's scornful disdain (perhaps his signature emotion) prompts him to some rather elaborate stylistic measures. The general shape is governed by what we might call "accumulation by repetition," an inventory of different respects in which Harding's writing is both boring and irritating. The first part is an extended anaphoric triplet: three "It reminds me"s, with a fourth implied before "of dogs." This is balanced by another four-sentence unit in the second part, all beginning with "It." Mencken's similes are striking: "wet sponges," "tattered washing," "stale bean soup," and "dogs barking." Harding's style then becomes active, as "grandeur creeps," his style "drags" and "crawls insanely"; and, as a result, it is judged to be "pishposh," "flapdoodle," and "balderdash," emphasized by separating the component parts of these expressions—"balder and dash"—which pretty much explains why Mencken is put off and why Harding's style is nothing short of revolting. Mencken is also, of course, depending on his readers' agreement that wet sponges, stale bean soup, and the rest are as disgusting as he thinks—which brings us back to the intimacy we talked about early on. And Harding would have to agree that these things are disgusting, too. So Mencken not only creates an artful insult here; he reads his audience correctly.

In Nancy McPhee's *The Book of Insults, Ancient and Modern* (New York, 1978) we find Algernon Swinburne (1837–1909) writing of Ralph Waldo Emerson, "A gap-toothed and hoary-headed ape . . . who now in his dotage spits and chatters from a dirtier perch of his own finding and fouling; coryphaeus or choragus of his Bulgarian tribe of autocoprophagous baboons" (14). Swinburne's image of Emerson and his admirers (an "ape" and "baboons") is enhanced by doublets ("gap-toothed and hoary-headed," "spits and chatters," and the alliterative "finding and fouling") and some elaborate diction ("coryphaeus" and "choragus," Greek words for "chorus leader"; and "autocoprophagous," which would "translate" as "those who eat their own shit," and who are, to boot, "Bulgarians"). Emerson was of course dead by the time Swinburne wrote this. But he would no doubt have understood even the most recherché of Swinburne's choice of words, and thus would have understood the insult were he around to read it. As far as audience intimacy is concerned, those whom Swinburne wanted to impress with his cleverness would have shared his attitude toward "autocaprophagous baboons." So here, too, preknowledge and agreement are preconditions for the success of the insult.

There is another insult in McPhee's collection that deserves attention, this one insulting boiled cabbage and, by extension, English cooking more generally. The writer is William Connor (1909–67), a well-known columnist known in the trade as Cassandra:

> Boiled cabbage *à l'Anglaise* is something compared with which steamed coarse newsprint bought from bankrupt Finnish salvage dealers and heated over smoky oil stoves is an exquisite delicacy. Boiled British cabbage is something lower than ex-Army blankets stolen by dispossessed Goanese doss-housekeepers who used them to cover busted-down hen houses in the slum area of Karachi, found them useless, threw them in anger into the Indus, where they were recovered by convicted beachcombers with grappling irons, who cut them in strips with shears and stewed them in sheep-dip before they were sold to dying beggars. Boiled cabbage! (29)

This is invective worthy of a Shakespeare—recall Hal in *Henry IV, Part 1* (1.2 and 2.4, for instance, as we saw earlier). Cassandra begins with a nauseating comparison, and then tops it with another, longer, one. What could be lower than a "dispossessed Goanese doss-housekeeper" (Indian Goa being a symbol of squalor; a "doss-housekeeper" a cleaner in a flophouse) and what more revolting than ex-Army blankets stewed in sheep-dip? What we are seeing here is also artistic in that it combines what Kenneth Burke calls (in the "Lexicon Rhetoricae" of *Counterstatement* [Los Altos, CA, 1953]) two kinds of "progressive form" ("form" defined as "the creation and fulfillment of expectations"): "qualitative progression" (we are put into a state of mind from which another state of mind can appropriately follow) and "repetitive form" (the restatement of a theme by new details). These necessarily overlap, Burke tells us (128–29), and Connor deploys them skillfully to keep us reading and to reach a (dyslogistic) climax, beyond which nothing can be lower.

The differences between insults like these and the exchanges we saw in the context of battle rap or, indeed, the polemics of Reformation-era Germany and France should be obvious. All three of the examples we have presented are characterized by attention to structure (or, for that matter, Burke's "form") and connection with both audience and designated insultee. And all three make ample use of the figures and tropes in the old rhetoric handbooks. In this respect, as previously noticed, they might also be compared to some of the epigrams of Martial; but in respect to magnitude and detail, they might also be compared to some of the passages from Cicero that we saw earlier, as well. In the end, given the "artistic," or aesthetic, character of these insults, we can appreciate them on their own artistic terms, quite aside from their intensity or effectiveness. And I dare say that if one were insulted in the way Mencken or Connor craft their insults, one would have to pause for a moment, before getting offended, to admire their skill.

Ad bellum purificandum?

We looked earlier at some of the consequences of legislating against insults and concluded that such legislation is not a very appealing idea. This is not to dismiss the importance of civility itself, surely a norm for constructive debate and an obviously desirable quality in any democratic process of decision making. But let us look again at civility.

Those who call for a return to "civility" and write up "codes of conduct" forbidding "hate speech" seem to think the world would be a better place without insults. I do not think that is necessarily the case, given the splendid examples of insults we just saw. Civility, in any case, when it is not just shallow cordiality, is frequently an appearance rather than a reality, a mask for motives more Machiavellian. And the norms of civility are far from absolute. I refer to John F. Kasson's illuminating *Rudeness and Civility* (New York, 1990), which relates the development of manuals laying down the rules of good manners during the nineteenth and early twentieth centuries. Kasson's book raises the question of who decides what "good manners" are? Who determines, as the authors of those manuals did, what the connection between manners and morals is? Is rudeness always a moral deficiency?

An argument might be made that a view of social interaction that pretends that status must be equally apportioned (for those manuals teach us how to identify with the class of "gentlemen and ladies"), that counsels "if you can't say anything nice, don't say anything at all," and that censors any speech that might be construed as a slur is a sterile and bland view indeed. More, it is historically ignorant, both in the sense that it knows little of the history of human relations and in the sense that it ignores what it does know.

A language without insults—to paraphrase what Agatha Christie once said about a kiss without a mustache—is like an egg without salt. It is hard to see, in any case, how insults could be removed from any language, since any word or phrase, under the right conditions, could be used or perceived as insulting. Many terms once considered abusive eventually lost their "edge" if they did not actually become terms of praise. Remove *psogos*—malediction—from the repertoire of rhetoric and you remove its counterpart, praise, as well; for the grounds of the put-down are the same as those of elevating an object of praise. Ancient writers on rhetoric were not just taking a shortcut when they observed that the commonplaces for derogation are merely the obverse of those for celebration.

It might be argued further that ridding the world of insults would be an unwarranted limitation to social interaction. After all, sometimes insults are in order—and we don't have to make up scenarios to support that proposition. Think of Aristophanes or Al Capp and their usually justified criticism of politicians, or even of the dozens. Sometimes the haughty need to be brought down, and sometimes the morally or intellectually deficient need to be reminded to keep their place. Say what you will about the nastiness of the Lutheran *Flugschriften*, but the fact remains that the cardinals and popes of the sixteenth century were hardly unsusceptible to luxuriance and vice. And say what you will about rude shopkeepers, but the fact remains that the customer is not always right. And, surely, rudeness in the face of rudeness is, if we agree with the principle of the just war, permitted and, indeed, appropriate.

On the other side, it must be allowed that insults can result in duels, riots, and even homicide. But one might observe that sensitivity to insult, and intensity of response to insult, are directly proportionate to one's sense of status and honor. Since some people have a strong sense of status, deservedly or not, and some people hold their honor as a possession not to be wasted, we might imagine that a world in which insults were unabashedly permitted would be one filled with conflict and even warfare. But this raises two questions. Would a world in which insults were forbidden be harmonious and peaceful? And isn't the real problem not with insults, as such, but with one's sense of status and honor? One could argue, I suppose, that the Poles, for instance, had good reason to take offense at satire in a German magazine, or that Judge Hoffman had good reason to object to the antics of the defendants (and their attorneys) in the Chicago Seven trial. But should satire be the cause of diplomatic crisis? And remember that Hoffman's charges of contempt of court were eventually reversed on appeal.

This brings us to another issue. Quite apart from questions raised by the notion of free speech, there may also be a problem with diagnostics. That is, prohibition of hate speech is often justified by an assertion that hate speech causes riots and unrest. Consider, for instance, the uproar after Benedict XVI, in the course of a talk he gave in Regensburg (in 2006), quoted a passage from the *Dialogue with a Turk* of the late-Byzantine emperor Manuel II Palaeologus (1350–1425) in which Manuel observes that Islam is a religion of violence. Islamists worldwide were enraged, and the consequence was more riots—not as violent as those following the publication of the Danish caricatures of Mohammed, but riots all the same. Was Benedict's "insult" the cause of that unrest, or simply the occasion—or excuse—for it? The Turks of Manuel's time would no doubt have dismissed Manuel's assertion as nonsense—or perhaps they would have gladly agreed. But it is doubtful that they would have been insulted. Islamists in today's Pakistan or Indonesia, however, deeply resentful of Western cultural hegemony and jealous of their own cultural status, perceived Benedict's statement—which was not, of course, his own expressed view—as a serious insult that called for response. But was rioting the proper response to the perceived insult? Why not a few insults in return? The riots were, I submit, simply statements of "Now you Westerners have gone too far"—"too far" in a long history of prejudice and oppression that happened long before Benedict XVI became pope, indeed, before he was born. Benedict's quotation from a long-dead Byzantine emperor was simply the excuse for doing what was in the works already, not the actual *cause* of the reaction. (Compare the cases of Pamuk and Shafak that we looked at earlier.)

Notice, too, the crucial importance of identification here. The reasoning of the Islamists seems to be that to insult Islam is to insult all Muslims—as indeed it is. The pope is identified not only with all Catholics, but with all Christians—perhaps with all non-Muslims. Here the paradox of which we also spoke seems to be absent, except that, obviously, both Benedict and the Muslims think violence is wrong. Benedict's response to the Muslim protestations pointed out that both religions are monotheistic, and so should be at peace with one another. No wonder, then, that Benedict's response was seen as irrelevant, for monotheism is not the issue.

I brought in, a little while ago, the matters of status and honor. We saw earlier that such practices as the dozens or the battle of wits at Versailles or, indeed, the political musings of Al Capp had much to do with what we called an "economy of scarcity" when it comes to status. When one seeks to assert or attain status in one's community, insults provide a means by way of put-downs of one's opponents in the scramble for recognition. Another way of asserting or attaining status that we saw earlier—albeit briefly—is by "detoxifying" terms of abuse: "Say it loud: I'm black and I'm proud," in the words of the late James Brown ("The Godfather of Soul"). Terms such as "slut" and "bitch" are appropriated by feminist extremists as positive images, not insulting terms. Unfortunately, this alternative was not available to Benedict (i.e., non-

Muslims) and the Muslims, both striving for status in the company of the virtuous. But notice that the Muslim response seems to have validated Manuel's assertion. There is no easy way to "detoxify" violence, and so, accordingly, it appears that non-Muslims are perceived as violent, too, as is attested by the invasion of Iraq, for instance. The only grounds for consubstantiality, then, would appear to be violence—a situation not very likely to provide any sort of resolution to the conflict. Benedict's choice of citation, then, however reasonable it may have been given his audience of seminarians at Regensberg, proved to be disastrous when reported to the Islamic press. It might, in short, be argued that it was Benedict's choice, and not Manuel's words, that was the cause—unintended, one might grant—of the unrest.

As for honor, it cannot be denied that in many cultures individual or group honor is strongly emphasized. Charles Flynn, whose book we had occasion to mention earlier, offers examples from a range of societies so varied as to include Prussian Junkers, Greek peasants, Texans, and the Tlingit on the Pacific Coast of North America. In all, the proper, and prescribed, reaction to any affront to one's honor is quick and violent retaliation. As he also notes, in such "touchy" societies, insults are often perceived where they were not intended. Nevertheless, *philotimo* (love of honor) is a powerful element in modern Greek society, for instance, and something very like it is equally powerful in Pakistan, Indonesia, and many other places. And we might add that "disrespect" is a common theme in battle rap as well as in everyday interactions in some settings in the Americas. Sometimes the nature of the retaliation is a matter of custom (as in the "honor killings" that have recently been reported as rampant in Pakistan and parts of India), and sometimes laid down in detailed legislation (as in the *Kanun* [code] of Lek in traditional Albania, the intricacies of which are explored in Ismail Kadare's novel *Broken April*). Perhaps this is what we were seeing in the response to Benedict's speech. One's sense of honor and its inviolability is clearly a function of one's status. The Junkers have honor; the peasants or shopkeepers of Prussia deserve no respect. And the severity of reaction is also tied up with status. As Aristotle notes in the *Rhetoric* (1.11, 1371a16–17), "no one pays attention to honor . . . accorded by those he much looks down upon, such as babies or uncivilized people." Conversely, as we've seen, affronts to one's honor by one's peers are paid close attention. But the most severe retaliations, it is true, are usually against insults by those of lower status. This is because insulters arrogate to themselves superiority, and those of actual higher status—hence, with more power—do not hesitate, in the interests of maintaining the hierarchy, to assert that status.

In the same chapter, Aristotle makes another interesting observation: "Honor and reputation are among the most pleasant things, through each person's imagining that he has the qualities of an important person" (1371a 8–9). The Greek word we have translated "imagining" is telling—*phantasia*; and "important person" is the English for the Greek *spoudaios*—"one who deserves to be taken seriously." Insults would constitute a threat to that "fantasy"—that is, a threat to what is popularly referred to as "self-esteem." But if we are talking here about self-esteem as a fantasy, one entertained even by those who are high up in the ranks of society, then perhaps their *philotimo* is less justifiable than they think. Bearing that possibility in mind might act as a reminder to those who feel insulted not to take themselves so seriously as to be offended even when no offense was intended, and it might also act as a check in the mind of the insulter, insofar as the insulter is arrogating to himself or herself a "fantasy" of deserving to be taken seriously.

The point is that prohibitions of certain types of speech or behavior would have unwelcome (because unintended?) consequences, and that the fundamental condition for true civility to thrive is that people not take themselves too seriously. More, if we are right in our observations on the "Islamic" response to Pope Benedict's speech, the real solution to the unrest it occasioned is not to forbid him to speak, but to alleviate the material and psychological conditions that cause the insulted party to respond so angrily and violently. It is not the insult that is the problem. Moreover, insults, whether real or not, will always be with us, just as hierarchy and identification will always be with us. What is called for is, again, not a code formulated by some Miss Manners, but a change of perspective and a consequent change of attitude.

We might take a hint from observations Kenneth Burke made in his *Rhetoric of Motives* to the effect that it is not always easy—or, indeed, possible—to distinguish clearly between "benign" persuasion and "malign" persuasion. "Epideictic," for instance (that most imprecise of labels), is generally agreed to be that genre of rhetoric in which communal values are celebrated—that is, it enacts the fundamental principle of identification. At the same time, "epideictic" (the opposite, recall, of *psogos*, or "vituperation") can be deployed, cynically, for advantage. It can be used as a way of talking someone into doing something or behaving in a certain way. This would be my reading of, for instance, Pliny's *Panegyric* of the emperor Trajan, but it is the same sort of thing as the praise given to a child as a means to encouraging good behavior—an approach school psychologists have recently dubbed "the nurtured heart." Epideictic (praise) can also be the vehicle for another kind of advantage, upward social mobility as in, for instance, the setting of the court of Louis XIV. It can be used, too, to create a false sense of self-esteem in the one being "praised," a deception aimed at setting the object of praise up for the big fall. Or think of the Homeric warrior who praises the man he has just killed (see *Iliad* 14.500ff., 20.389ff.), where posthumous praise is in fact a form of put-down. More generally, even the kind of rhetoric that Wayne Booth celebrates in *The Rhetoric of Rhetoric* (Oxford: Blackwell, 2004) as "listening rhetoric," in which "both sides join in a trusting dispute, determined to listen to the opponent's argument . . . pursuing not just victory but . . . new agreement about what is real" (46–47), has a dark side, a shoddy version of "win rhetoric" (mere eristic) that Booth calls "surrender rhetoric": one side *pretends* to have been persuaded in order to prevail.

Conversely, what Booth might have characterized as a prime example of "win rhetoric," the put-down or denigration designed to demonstrate the inferiority of one's opponent (i.e., insult), can be seen as having a benign side. As we have observed, one side of insult calls for shared values and beliefs, rests on a kind of intimacy between insulter and the one being insulted, and can be a way of reinforcing social bonds, not just asserting alienation. Insults can be viewed as indirect celebrations of public virtue and as an implicit recognition of the ubiquity of hierarchy. And insults can be a method of motivating people to do their best—what, I suppose, we might call "the noble insult," like the "noble lie" in Plato or Quintilian. Finally, insults can be a powerful mode of truth-telling. Mencken speaks the truth to Harding's "eloquence," and it might be argued that Cicero's *Second Philippic* spoke the truth to Antony's fitness to lead the Roman republic.

Things, in short, are not as simple as they might seem. Praise and insult are not as clearly opposite to one another as they are commonly believed to be. And if we see—if we'd care to notice—that insult is not simply a means of encouraging enmity and disdain, we'd be able to regard it as an interesting and important aspect of human relations as viewed from a rhetorical perspective, and not as a social or moral failing, as it is also commonly held to be.

A Parting Shot

In the spring of 1501, workers in Rome, in the course of repaving part of the Piazza Navona, dug up a battered ancient statue close to the Palazzo Braschi. They named it Pasquino (it was the Easter season) and set it upright. Before long, the torso was draped in a sort of toga and neighborhood people began to attach scraps of paper with satiric epigrams written on them critical of local politicians and, indeed, of the pope himself. These were, of course, anonymous, as personal attacks were forbidden. These epigrams, a record of the people's dissatisfactions and denouncements of the injustices they saw, came to be known as *pasquinate*. Thus Pasquino became the first of Rome's "talking statues." (On this, see Roberto Piperno's "The Talking Statues of Rome," at http://www.romeartlover.it/Talking.html.) Before long, other statues appeared on the scene, also festooned with epigrams—statues with names like *Abate Luigi*, *Madamma Lucrezia*, *Il Faccino* (The Joker), and *Il Babuino* (The Baboon). Collectively, they made up what the locals referred to a *Congresso degli Arguti*, the Congress of Wits. This is the origin of the word *pasquinade*, "an anonymous lampoon, whether in verse or prose." Long live Pasquino!

NOTES ON FURTHER READING

In addition to the works already cited in this volume, there are several that bear more or less directly on what we have been saying about insult. I will restrict myself to books and articles in English. Jonathon Green's *Words Apart: The Language of Prejudice* (London, 1996) covers an enormous range of abusive terminology. Robert M. Adams makes some penetrating observations on insult in his "Invective and Insult," in *Bad Mouth: Fugitive Papers on the Dark Side* (Berkeley, 1977), 21–42. Edmund Leach's well-known "Anthropological Aspects of Language: Animal Categories and Verbal Abuse," originally published in *New Directions in the Study of Language*, ed. E. Lennenberg (Boston, 1964), 23–63 (reprinted in *Mythology: Selected Readings*, ed. P. Maranda [Baltimore, 1973], 39–67) traces norms of abuse to beliefs in taboos, thus providing one explanation of how terms become culturally specific terms of abuse. Judith T. Irvine's "Insult and Responsibility: Verbal Abuse in a Wolof Village," in *Responsibility and Evidence in Oral Discourse*, ed. J. Hill and J. T. Irvine (Cambridge, 1993), 105–34, discusses the multiplicity of factors an anthropologist needs to consider in assessing verbal abuse. The section devoted to "cursing and insults" in Gershom Legman's *Rationale of the Dirty Joke* (New York, 1975) is disappointingly thin (barely thirty pages, 779–89), though certainly not uninformative. Laura Gowing is particularly interested in the differences between male and female insults in her "Gender and the Language of Insult in Early Modern London," in *History Workshop* 35 (1993): 1–22.

Stephen Halliwell's "Aischrology, Shame, and Comedy," in *Free Speech in Classical Antiquity*, ed. I. Sluiter and R. Rosen (Boston, 2004), 115–44, addresses the limits on abuse in fifth-century Athens. See also Susanna Morton Braund, in the same collection of essays (409–28), "*Libertas* or *Licentia*? Freedom and Criticism in Roman Satire," where she makes some tantalizing (but not very persuasive) comparisons between the satires of Juvenal and Horace and the strategies used by Eminem. A similar argument is made by Ralph M. Rosen and Donald R. Marks in "Comedies of Transgression in Gangsta Rap and Ancient Classical Poetry," in *New Literary History* 30 (1999): 897–928. Rosen and Marks, however, argue that the genre shared by such performers as Eminem, Aristophanes, and Horace "operates according to principles that are conceptually prior to an author's lived reality" (897), and so are working at a very high level of abstraction indeed. I have looked at fourth-century materials in my "Topics of Vituperation: Some Commonplaces of 4th Century Oratory," in *Influences on Peripatetic Rhetoric*, ed. D. Mirhady (Leiden, 2007), 231–338. Anthony Corbeill's "Ciceronian Invective," in *Brill's Companion to Cicero: Oratory and Rhetoric*, ed. J. May (Boston, 2002), 197–218, provides an interesting overview; but see also, in the same volume (159–96), Andrew M. Riggsby's "The *Post Reditum* Speeches," especially at 179–82.

On religious vituperation, see, e.g., L. Racaut, *Hatred in Print: Catholic Propaganda and Protestant Identity During the French Wars of Religion* (Aldershot, 2002); J. Sawyer, *Printed Poison: Pamphlet Propaganda, Faction Politics, and the Public Sphere in Early Seventeenth- Century France* (Berkeley, 1990); and my "Vituperation in Early Seventeenth Century Historical Studies," *Rhetorica* 22 (2004): 169–82. A vast array of engravings found in sixteenth-century *Flugschriften* can be seen in the four volumes of Max Geisberg's *The German Single-leaf Woodcut, 1500–1550*, ed. W. Srauss (New York, 1974). Some of the essays in *Subversion and Scurrility: Popular Discourse in Europe from 1500 to the Present*, ed. D. Cavanagh and T. Kirk (Burlington, VT, 2000) bear particularly on our observations on religious invective and the interrogation of hierarchies. See, for instance, Dermot Cavanagh's "Skelton and Scurrility" (26–41) and Gerhard Ammerer's "The Last Austrian-Turkish War (1788–9) and Public Opinion in Vienna" (138–56, with illustrations).

The classic study of the dozens is Willam Labov, "Rituals for Insults," in *Language in the Inner City: Studies in the Black English Vernacular* (Philadelphia, 1972), 297–353. One topic (of many) we did not discuss is the tradition of "flyting," insult poetry. A good introduction, especially to the Scottish tradition, can be found in Priscilla Bawcutt's book on the Scots poet William Dunbar (d. ca. 1520), *Dunbar the Makar* (Oxford, 1992), 220–56. For the texts, see J. Kinsley's edition, *The Poems of William Dunbar* (Oxford, 1979), which contains a lengthy glossary for those who do not read Scots. Less interesting, but still informative, is Karen Swenson's study of Old Norse insults in *Performing Definitions: Two Genres of Insult in Old Norse Literature*, Studies in Scandinavian Literature and Culture 3 (Columbia, SC, 1991).

Linda Hutcheon's *Irony's Edge: The Theory and Politics of Irony* (New York, 1994) finds in irony the same sort of paradox—that it is both aggregative and divisive—as we saw in insults. The papers collected in M. J. Matsuda et al., *Words That Wound: Critical Race Theory, Assaultive Speech and the First Amendment* (Boulder, 1993), and Judith Butler's *Excitable Speech: A Politics of the Performative* (New York, 1997) bear directly on our observations of hate speech, but stress perhaps too much the usefulness of Speech Act theory. The essays in J. Peristiani, ed., *Honor and Shame: The Values of Mediterranean Society* (Chicago, 1966), including one by Pierre Bourdieu, are useful reading, as are those in D. Gilmore, ed., *Honor and Shame and the Unity of the Mediterranean* (Washington DC, 1987).

The recent collection in Donald Dewey's *The Art of Ill Will: American Political Cartoons* (New York, 2007) includes many from the early nineteenth century as well as more recent ones (which pale by comparison).

J. M. Coetzee's essays in *Giving Offense: Essays on Censorship* (Chicago, 1996) are required reading. Jerome Neu's *Sticks and Stones: The Philosophy of Insults* (New York) came out after the present book was finished. While he has much of interest to say about the legal angle on perceived insults, his treatment is overly dependent on Freud, the most often cited authority in the book

And finally, Pasquino had, as it happens, a long life—in England, for instance, from Thomas Elyot's *Pasquil the Playne* (1533) to Henry Fielding's *Pasquin* (1736)—that has yet to be chronicled.

INDEX

Aristophanes, 3, 106–9, 113, 121, 128
    Acharnians, 3, 108–9
    Knights, 106–9, 113
Aristotle, 81, 99–100, 123, 124
Ass-Pope, 72, 74

battle rap, 89, 108, 119, 123
Benedict XVI, 121–23
Booth, Wayne C., 28, 125
Burke, Kenneth, vii, 7, 67, 77–78, 119, 124

Capp, Al, 84, 101, 107, 121, 122
Chaucer, Geoffrey, 26
Chicago Seven, 5, 121
Cicero, 31–42, 49, 78–79
    In Pisonem, 33, 38
    Second Catalinarian, 33
    Second Phillipic, 34, 38, 39, 125
civility, v, 2, 63, 113–14, 119, 120, 124
Cohen, Ted, 28, 67, 68

Dozens, 3, 87–91, 94, 97–99, 116, 121

Édouard, Robert, 9–10, 12, 16
Eminem, 18, 21, 89–90, 94, 98, 117
Erasmus, 109–12
ethnicity and nationality, 14, 18

Falstaff, 16, 50–54, 56–59
females, 9, 17–18
Flugschriften, 71–72, 73, 76, 78, 84, 98, 101, 121
Ford, Henry, 106

gestures, 7, 22–25, 27, 66, 91

hate speech, 21, 113, 120–21
hierarchy, 87, 101, 105–6, 109, 113, 124

identification, 69, 98–99
irony, 28, 109

jokes, 28, 67–69

Kennedy, Randall, 21

Lawrence, D. H., 26
Luther, Martin, 70–71, 73, 110

Martial, 40–49, 58, 94, 98, 101, 117, 119
    Epigrams
        1.80, 42
        1.81, 41
        1.83, 43
        1.92, 47
        2.89, 42
        3.66, 41
        5.69, 42
        7.20, 41, 43–44, 47, 48
        9.27, 45
        9.57, 46, 48
        11.20, 42
Mencken, H. L., 117, 118, 125
Monty Python, 61, 64, 66, 69, 80, 84, 94, 97

Nabokov, Vladimir, 23

paradox of insult, 97–98
Pasquino, 126
political cartoons, 8, 12, 78
Protocols of the Elders of Zion, 102, 105

Ridicule, 92–93
Roman comedy, 14, 17, 39
Rove, Karl, 78

Scaliger, J. C., 48, 109–12
Shakespeare, William, 16, 50–62 passim, 66, 69, 84, 108
   Coriolanus, 16
   Henry IV, Part I, 50–52
   Henry IV, Part II, 53–54
   Henry V, 55

King Lear, 16
Merry Wives of Windsor, 54, 56–61 passim, 69, 108
Much Ado about Nothing, 16
Romeo and Juliet, 23, 55
Shakespeare Insult Kit, 15, 50, 61, 94
shame and honor, 99–100, 121, 123
stock topics (loci), 41, 43–46 passim, 58, 61, 63, 84, 94, 97, 99
Streicher, Julius, 101–2, 105–6, 113

terms of abuse, 7, 9–13 passim, 17, 24–26 passim, 39, 61–62, 71–72, 94, 114, 122

whore of Babylon, 70–71, 75